D1190805

Mormon Crisis
Anatomy of a Failing Religion
James A. Beverley

CASTLE QUAY BOOKS

Mormon Crisis: Anatomy of a Failing Religion

Copyright ©2013 James A Beverley
All rights reserved
Printed in Canada

International Standard Book Number: 978-1-927355-32-9
ISBN 978-1-927355-33-6 EPUB

Published by:
Castle Quay Books
Pickering, Ontario, L1W 1A5
Tel: (416) 573-3249
E-mail: info@castlequaybooks.com
www.castlequaybooks.com

Edited by Larry Matthews and Lori MacKay
Cover design by Burst Impressions
Printed at Essence Publishing, Belleville, Ontario

Scripture quotations marked NIV are taken from the HOLY BIBLE, NEW INTERNATIONAL VERSION ®. Copyright © 1973, 1978, 1984 by International Bible Society. Used by permission of Zondervan Publishing House. All rights reserved. Scripture quotations marked KJV are from The Holy Bible, King James Version. Copyright © 1977, 1984, Thomas Nelson Inc., Publishers. All rights reserved. Scripture quotations marked NKJV are taken from the New King James Version. Copyright © 1979, 1980, 1982. Thomas Nelson Inc., Publishers.

This book or parts thereof may not be reproduced in any form without prior written permission of the publishers.

Library and Archives Canada Cataloguing in Publication
Beverley, James A.

     The Mormon crisis: anatomy of a failing religion / James A. Beverley ; foreword by Sandra Tanner.
Includes bibliographical references.
Issued also in electronic format.

ISBN 978-1-927355-32-9

     1. Mormon Church—History. 2. Church of Jesus Christ of Latter-day Saints—Doctrines. I. Title.

BX8611.B49 2013   289.309   C2013-901387-3

To my uncle Bill

(William Edward Bulman, 1920-)

Your dedication in fighting for freedom in World War II, your love for family and friends, and your faithful witness to Jesus Christ is an inspiration

Contents

Foreword...7

Preface 9

The Mormon Story 15

Joseph Smith and the First Vision 25

The Prophet and Buried Treasure................................35

Those Many Wives..43

The Church and the Prophets 51

The Book of Mormon...63

Doctrine and Covenants...75

The Pearl of Great Price...83

The Book of Abraham 93

God and Many Gods 103

Jesus, Holy Spirit and Humanity................................113

The Temple and the Secrets 123

Blacks and the Priesthood..135

Conclusions 145

Postscript..155

APPENDIX MATERIAL

Mountain Meadows Massacre.......................................157

Evangelicals and the LDS 161

Modern Mormon Polygamy 165

Timeline of Mormonism 169

Resources for Further Study...175
Recommended Reading 177
Endnotes..179

Foreword

"Sandra, that's blasphemy," replied the eighth grade Christian girl in response to my teenage attempt to explain LDS theology. The LDS quote I had repeated to her was the famous couplet by past LDS President Lorenzo Snow: "As man now is, God once was; As God now is, man may be."[1] It wasn't until several years later, after giving my life to Christ, that I realized the truth of my friend's assessment.

There have been many changes in the Mormon world since that day in the 1950s, but much remains the same. Over the next 50 plus years my husband and I, both from fifth generation LDS families, published extensively on the historical and doctrinal changes of the LDS Church that led us to reject the religion of our childhood and embrace Christianity as revealed in the Bible.[2]

In 1978 the LDS president announced a reversal of their ban on blacks holding their priesthood, yet their past racism continues to haunt them. And in recent years the LDS leaders have modified their teaching manuals to obscure their more heretical doctrines, such as God was once a mortal and achieved his present status of godhood after years of diligent effort. In 1971 their official church magazine, *Ensign*[3], published Joseph Smith's famous sermon on the nature of God. However, in recent years there have been only brief quotes from his sermon in their literature. For a while Lorenzo Snow's couplet seemed to be pushed into the background, yet their 2013 priesthood manual, *Teachings of Presidents of the Church: Lorenzo Snow*, highlights his statement. In 1843 Joseph Smith introduced the secret LDS temple ritual, where couples are sealed in marriage for all eternity. But since 1900 the ritual has gone through various revisions. The history behind these events shows an ongoing effort to present the LDS claims in the most favorable light and to obscure the distinctions between biblical Christianity and LDS theology.

Professor Beverley and I first connected in 1978 when he began teaching on Mormonism. Over the years I have shared research material with him and helped him get connected to other Christian scholars of Mormonism, including Wes Walters and H. Michael Marquardt. As Mormonism extends its world-wide proselytizing efforts, with 55,000 young people serving two year missions, it is important that Christians understand and know how to respond to LDS claims. Professor Beverley's book is a welcome addition to the research on Mormonism. His book offers the reader an up-to-date, powerful and accurate critique of Mormonism.

Sandra Tanner
Co-founder Utah Lighthouse Ministry

Preface

Mitt Romney's run for President of the United States in 2012 was the main reason behind what was called the "Mormon Moment." Could Romney, a Mormon, become the head of the most powerful nation on earth? In the end, Romney lost but the close election proved that his Mormon faith was not a barrier to millions of Americans. Overall, members of the Church of Jesus Christ of Latter-day Saints were proud of him and LDS leaders used the election as a context for renewed explanation and defense of the Mormon gospel.

The Mormon Moment has passed but there remains a need for careful analysis of the Latter-day Saints beliefs and practices. The intense focus on Mormonism through Romney's two campaigns for political leadership led to more heat than light. Much of the discussion on Mormonism lacked depth. Romney himself seldom got into details about his Mormon faith. As well, the LDS public relations machine often glossed over serious issues in Mormon history and belief.

The American evangelical Christian community was torn by how to react to Romney and Mormonism. Many evangelicals are Republican so wanted to vote for him but had serious concerns about Mormonism. This reached a telling moment when famed evangelist Billy Graham showed his support for Romney, followed by the removal of an entry on Mormonism as a cult from the website of the Billy Graham Evangelistic Association.

The win by Obama resulted in an instant quiet about Mormonism in the public square. However, the need for an up-to-date appraisal is urgent. First, contrary to popular impression, the LDS Church is in trouble in terms of growth and members leaving the Church. Second, the Mormon moment created uncertainty among evangelicals about the proper reaction to the LDS belief system. Is it Christian? Are Mormons spiritual brothers and sisters in Christ to Protestant, Catholic and Orthodox Christians? Is the Mormon Church becoming more evangelical, more attuned to the Bible and more Christ-centered?

The 2012 election season gave me the opportunity to return in a deeper way to my longtime study of Mormonism. I became interested in the LDS religion when I was studying at Trinity Evangelical Divinity School in 1976 in a class with Norman Geisler. I became a professor in 1978 and analysis of Mormonism became part of my regular teaching and has continued ever since. Different trips to Utah over the years have given me a chance to examine the LDS religion in its home base. One of those trips involved my coverage of Ravi Zacharias' famous and controversial speech at the Mormon Tabernacle.

The LDS Church is in serious trouble. That explains my book title: Mormon Crisis and the subtitle: Anatomy of a Failing Religion. The troubles in the Mormon faith relate to two major realities. First, as chapter one notes, the Internet has created a huge problem for Mormonism because of the abundance of powerful and effective critique of the LDS religion. Second, and far more important, in spite of the phenomenal growth of the LDS Church in the twentieth century, huge defects in the Mormon belief system remain, as this book documents.

Anyone who studies the LDS Church cannot but help be impressed by many facets of the Mormon story and by many great elements in Mormon culture. Many ex-Mormons express their agony over leaving behind the wonderful support system that the Mormon community provides. The LDS Church offers a cohesive framework of faith set in the context of a powerful missionary force, a vast educational system, and worldwide relief network. The men who run the LDS empire have built up an astonishing array of temples, churches, educational institutes, and business interests. So, whatever concerns this book raises are set in the context of admiration for much about the LDS faith and especially deep appreciation for the many wonderful LDS people that I have met.

Readers will notice that I have chosen not to enter the debate about the use of the word cult to describe Mormonism. The reason for this is two-fold. First, as a matter of diplomacy, why use such a nasty word in a book that invites Mormons to really consider my investigation of major Mormon beliefs and claims? Second, there are such serious issues to work on in this book that I have decided to leave the use of the cult word to another time and place.

I leave to the end of the book some consideration of how I think the term Christian should be used of the Latter-day Saint Church. In the main text I refer to traditional Christian views as a way of a contrast with Mormonism. This would seem to suggest that Mormonism is non-traditional Christianity but still Christianity. Again, I will address that in the book's conclusion. For now let me suggest that I think debate about whether Mormonism is Christian should give way to focus on specific doctrines and issues that divide Mormons and evangelicals. Otherwise, things get lost in heated debates over whether someone is "really" a Christian or if Mormons and evangelicals follow the "same" God or the "same" Jesus.

I realize that my evangelical Christian perspective will create tensions at certain points with others, Mormons and otherwise. My criticisms of the LDS Church and certain of its leaders and ideas are offered with a deep recognition of my own fallibility. Consequently, I welcome input on what I have written though I also ask for civility in dialogue.

Like any author, I also hope that readers will grant me benefit of the doubt as regards motives and basic decency. When I offer negative verdicts at many points it is not done in malice or in any sense of hate. Whatever critique is offered is done because I believe that it is both true and necessary. It is not my intention to minimize the good in Mormonism. Likewise, critique is not meant to support those who crush religious liberties related to the LDS world or endorse nasty, bizarre and false theories about Mormonism.

Working on this book over the last year has left me in debt to a number of individual scholars who have helped in my investigation. In particular, I am grateful to Sandra Tanner for many hours of conversation and for writing the foreword to this book. Likewise, I have learned much from Tom Kimball, Michael Marquardt, Dan Vogel, Grant Palmer, Pichard Packham, Newell Bringhurst, Bill McKeever, Frank Beckwith, Ross Anderson, and Will Bagley. Going back to other years, conversations with Greg Johnson, Craig Hazen, Norman Geisler, Craig Blomberg, the late Wes Walters, Carl Mosser, Kevin and Jill Rische, Ravi

Zacharias, Ron Huggins, the late Walter Martin, Gerald McDermott, and Richard Mouw have been very rewarding. I have also had stimulating conversations with various Mormon leaders and scholars. Since I do not want any of them to be burdened by a connection to various criticisms of Mormonism in this book, they will remain nameless. You know who you are and I am immensely grateful for the opportunity of interaction.

I owe much to a circle of friends who have provided at different times encouragement in my life and work. So, thanks to John and Trish Wilkinson, Marta Durski, Annie McKeown Bain, Gary and Peg LeBlanc, Kevin and Sandy Quast, Rodney and Adonica Howard-Browne, John Axler, Larry and Beverly Matthews, Carol Greig, Rick and Darlene George, Stephen and Dawn Stultz, Sharon Geldart, Doug and Pat Markle, Larry Willard, Ken and Miriam MacLeod, Ralston and Cheryl Nickerson, John and Teresa Reddy, Tom Dikens, Randy and Cindy McCooeye, Sam Mikolaski, Bob and Mary Gunn, Norm Keith, Kevin and Jill Rische, Dave Collison, Rick and Charis Tobias, Bryan and Jeannie Taylor, Jerry and Karen Reddy, the late Clark Pinnock, Rick Love, Gladys Chan, Gary Habermas, Bruxy and Nina Cavey, Mike Homer, Ann Young and her late husband Bob, Daveed Gartenstein-Ross, Terry and Berry Trites, Pat Minichello, Reg and Linda Horsman, Phil Sherwood, Wade Wry, Randy and Susan Campbell, Jim Penton, Cheryl Geissler, and Bill and Mary-Lynne Rout.

I also want to acknowledge the influence of several academics in my life. Eileen Barker, Massimo Introvigne, Todd Johnson, Don Wiebe, and Gordon Melton, are valued friends and constant sources of learning about the world of religion, even when we disagree. Since 2003 I have worked with Gordon as Associate Director of his Institute for the Study of American Religion. In 2007 I became friends with the late Martin Gardner, the famous author, and his interest in my work has been wonderful. I am also grateful for continuing encouragement from Hans Küng, my former professor during Ph.D. work at the Toronto School of Theology. His breadth of learning and courage in theological life is a source of inspiration.

Tyndale Seminary has been my academic home since 1988. I am grateful to Tyndale administration for their support: Gary Nelson, Janet Clark, Winston Ling, and Randy Henderson. Thanks also to Brian Stiller,

Ian Rennie and Brian Cunnington for their enthusiasm and interest in my work. All of my faculty colleagues over the years have been supportive but a special nod to John Kessler, David Sherbino, Victor Shepherd, and Kaarina Hsieh. Thanks also to Andrew Smith and Toby Goodman for their help in the world of computing. I owe a lot to current and former administrative assistants, including Tina Kim, Dahlia Fraser, Cathy Nguyen, Betty Poon, Esther Kim, and Lynda Marshall.

I am very grateful to several friends who have provided academic assistance and help in research in times past and present: Agnes Choi, Ann Stocker, Rachel Collins, Darren Hewer, Chad Hillier, Brett Potter and Rebekka Ries. Some of the material in this book first saw light in magazine format. Thanks to *Christianity Today* editors David Neff and Mark Galli for their support and the same thanks to Gail Reid and Bill Fledderus at *Faith Today* magazine.

I am surrounded by a great circle of relatives, including Bill Bulman, Reta Lutes, Norman and Phyllis Gillcash, Jack and Grace Stultz, David and Darlene Keirstead, Gerry and Judy Gillcash, Cindy Beverley, James A. Beverley (my namesake) and Mary Jo Beverley, Lorne and Linda Gillcash, Bill and Nancy Bulman, and Keith and Mary Beverley. My twin brother Bob Beverley is a constant source of love and enthusiasm. As ever, and most important, I am so grateful to my immediate family: my wife Gloria, our adult children, Derek and Andrea, and Julien, our son-in-law. And, I remain grateful to God for Dorothée and Ari, our two wonderful grandchildren.

James A. Beverley
Professor of Christian Thought and Ethics
Tyndale Seminary, Toronto, Canada
Associate Director
Institute for the Study of American Religion
Beaumont, Texas
April 2013
jamesbeverley@sympatico.ca
www.jamesbeverley.com

The Mormon Story

The growth of the Church of Jesus Christ of Latter-day Saints is one of the amazing realities of religion in the last two centuries. Joseph Smith, the Mormon prophet, founded the Mormon Church in 1830. There were six members. Today there are over 5 million members in the United States, part of a worldwide membership of 14.5 million.[1] The first meeting took place in one home in New York State.[2] Today members gather in over 28,000 congregations in 177 countries.

A New Prophet for a New Church

The story of Mormonism hinges around a controversial nineteenth-century man named Joseph Smith, Jr. He was born on December 23, 1805, in Sharon, Vermont, but moved with his family to Palmyra, New York, in 1816. Joseph's family and other area residents were divided over which church to join. Mormons believe that Joseph prayed about the matter and on a spring day in 1820 both God the Father and Jesus appeared to Joseph Smith and told him to restore the one true church. This episode is called the "First Vision" story and constitutes one of the most important historic claims of Mormonism.[3]

Mormons also believe that Smith continued to receive supernatural revelation. On September 21, 1823 an angel named Moroni told him of gold plates that were buried in the hill Cumorah near Palmyra. Smith was denied permission to get the plates until the same date in 1827. Earlier that year Smith married Emma Hale. Their first two years of marriage were taken up with getting the plates, translating them and then getting the book published. The result was the release of The Book of Mormon in March 1830. Smith claimed that the gold plates contained the record of Jewish groups who settled in the Americas around 600 B.C. Early converts were drawn to Smith and The Book of Mormon but the Latter-day Saints also received opposition from traditional Christians.

Some Mormons settled in Ohio in 1831 and others moved further west to Missouri. Mormons believe that Smith continued to receive divine guidance. His revelations were recorded in the Book of Commandments in 1833 and then later in Doctrine and Covenants. Mormons continued to be persecuted, especially in Missouri. This came in part because of Mormon claims about God promising that they would take over Jackson County. Smith also proclaimed that Independence, Missouri, would be the site of the New Jerusalem predicted in the Book of Revelation. Smith himself was arrested there in 1838 during the "Mormon Wars" but escaped custody in 1839.[4] Smith then built a new Mormon community in Nauvoo, in the northwest part of Illinois.

During the early 1840s Smith was the object of both internal dissent and external criticism, particularly regarding the practice of plural marriage. In June 1844 Smith was jailed in Carthage, Illinois, on charges of ordering the destruction of a newspaper called the *Nauvoo Expositor*, a paper started by William Law, a leading ex-Mormon. Law had circulated the view that Smith believed in many gods and practiced polygamy. Before coming to trial Smith and his brother Hyrum were killed by an angry anti-Mormon mob on June 27, 1844.

The Move to a New Frontier

The early Mormons were devastated by the killing of their prophet. His death brought despair and confusion to the young church. Various Mormon elders vied for leadership, including James J. Strang, Sidney Rigdon, and Brigham Young. In the end, most Mormons chose to follow Brigham Young, who was head of the Quorum of the Twelve Apostles. Young helped to stabilize the Mormons but persecutions started again and Young decided to lead the Mormons westward.[v] Most Mormons who stayed behind followed either Strang or Rigdon or eventually joined the Reorganized Church of Latter-day Saints, now known as the Community of Christ.

Young left with a small company on February 1846. Soon after thousands of Mormons followed in long wagon trains in what is probably the greatest migration in American history. Young's group climbed the last incline and saw the great Salt Lake Basin on July 24, 1847. Young wrote in his journal: "The spirit of light rested on us and hovered over the valley, and I felt that there the Saints would find protection and safety."[6] Young, often called the American Moses, was declared the second prophet of the Church on December 27, 1847. He became the first governor of Utah and led the LDS Church until his death on August 29, 1877.[7]

Young's leadership was not without its problems and controversies. Utah was declared a USA territory in 1850 but relations between Young and the federal government collapsed later in the decade. James Buchanan, elected U.S. President in 1857, ordered U.S. soldiers to Utah the same year. This provocation led to the Utah War, largely a non-violent standoff between Mormon militia and the U.S. Army that lasted from the summer of 1857 until April of 1858.

One of the darkest episodes in Mormon history took place in the context of the Utah War. On September 11, 1857 a group of 120 settlers from Arkansas were killed while traveling through southern Utah on their way to California. This has become known as the Mountain Meadows Massacre. Brigham Young implicated Indians in the murders but the massacre was the work of Mormon militants, under the leadership of John D. Lee. Though Young was never directly implicated in the massacre, there is reason to believe that he helped set the stage for one of the largest mass murders in American history.[8]

The Polygamy Issue

Brigham Young led Mormons in their first public advocacy and practice of plural marriage. The doctrine was officially sanctioned in 1852 though Joseph Smith claimed to receive a private revelation on polygamy in 1843. As we will note later, Smith had many plural wives and he set the pattern for other LDS leaders, including Young. The U.S. government turned a blind eye to polygamy during Young's presidency but pressure increased after his death, especially with the passing of the Edmunds-Tucker Act of 1887. This Act gave the U.S. government the power to take over all church assets as a result of continued practice of polygamy.

The federal pressure against polygamy led Mormon president

Wilford Woodruff to issue a manifesto against polygamy in 1890. This compromise with the federal government led to Utah's admission to statehood in 1896. While some LDS leaders continued to sanction plural marriages privately, within two decades it became clear that the LDS Church would no longer support those Saints who chose that path. The Woodruff Manifesto reads in part:

> Inasmuch as laws have been enacted by Congress forbidding plural marriages, which laws have been pronounced constitutional by the court of last resort, I hereby declare my intention to submit to those laws, and to use my influence with the members of the Church over which I preside to have them do likewise. There is nothing in my teachings to the Church or in those of my associates, during the time specified, which can be reasonably construed to inculcate or encourage polygamy; and when any Elder of the Church has used language which appeared to convey any such teaching, he has been promptly reproved. And I now publicly declare that my advice to the Latter-day Saints is to refrain from contracting any marriage forbidden by the law of the land.[9]

Post-Manifesto LDS history

The twentieth century brought the LDS Church into mainstream America. As polygamy moved further from regular LDS life, the Church expanded its missionary force, increased its focus on family living, Temple rituals, and relief work.

The most significant change in the modern LDS story came in 1978 when Mormon prophet Spencer W. Kimball ended the ban on blacks holding the priesthood. This change was heralded in front-page news stories all over the world and earned the LDS Church greater respect among non-Mormons. Contrary to what some critics argue, the evidence clearly suggests that Kimball did not make the change for pragmatic reasons alone but felt that the radical change in policy was mandated to him by God.

In 1995 the First Presidency and the Quorum of the Twelve released "The Family: A Proclamation to the World." This document affirmed traditional family values and anchored marriage and family in the will of God. "Marriage between man and woman is essential to His eternal plan. Children are entitled to birth within the bonds of matrimony, and to be reared by a father and a mother who honor marital vows with complete fidelity."[10] The conservative nature of Mormonism was evident in the proclamation and coincided with longstanding objections to feminism and gay rights, two issues that have grown in significance in the last three decades.

Salt Lake City was chosen as the base for the 2002 Winter Olympics. This not only brought the LDS faith to the attention of a watching world but introduced Mitt Romney to an international audience. In his later bid for the 2008 Republican nomination and in the 2012 Presidential run Romney staunchly defended his Mormon faith. While he avoided getting into specific debates about Mormon history or doctrine, he also refused to minimize his personal belief in the LDS Gospel. In his 2007 "Faith in America" address, Romney declared: "I believe in my Mormon faith and I endeavor to live by it. My faith is the faith of my fathers – I will be true to them and to my beliefs." He went on to say that he is often asked his belief about Jesus and stated: "I believe that Jesus Christ is the Son of God and the Savior of mankind."[11]

Romney is joined by over 14 million Latter-day Saints worldwide who believe that God restored the Gospel to the earth through a prophet named Joseph Smith. The Saints believe that the Church of Jesus Christ of Latter-day Saints is the "one true Church" on the earth and that this Church has been led by prophets since its founding in 1830. The Church today has over 50,000 missionaries spreading the message of a restored Gospel that they believe was originally given by Jesus Christ two thousand years ago.

The LDS message

The LDS understanding of the Christian gospel is presented in the Articles of Faith, originally written by Joseph Smith in 1842. The Articles contain items typical of the Protestant world of Smith's upbringing but also provide unique LDS expressions on various doctrines.

1. We believe in God, the Eternal Father, and in His Son, Jesus Christ, and in the Holy Ghost.

2. We believe that men will be punished for their own sins, and not for Adam's transgression.

3. We believe that through the Atonement of Christ, all mankind may be saved, by obedience to the laws and ordinances of the Gospel.

4. We believe that the first principles and ordinances of the Gospel are: first, Faith in the Lord Jesus Christ; second, Repentance; third, Baptism by immersion for the remission of sins; fourth, Laying on of hands for the gift of the Holy Ghost.

5. We believe that a man must be called of God, by prophecy, and by the laying on of hands by those who are in authority, to preach the Gospel and administer in the ordinances thereof.

6. We believe in the same organization that existed in the Primitive Church, namely, apostles, prophets, pastors, teachers, evangelists, and so forth.

7. We believe in the gift of tongues, prophecy, revelation, visions, healing, interpretation of tongues, and so forth.

8. We believe the Bible to be the word of God as far as it is translated correctly; we also believe The Book of Mormon to be the word of God.

9. We believe all that God has revealed, all that He does now reveal, and we believe that He will yet reveal many great and important things pertaining to the Kingdom of God.

10. We believe in the literal gathering of Israel and in the restoration of the Ten Tribes; that Zion (the New Jerusalem) will be built upon the American continent; that Christ will reign personally upon the earth; and, that the earth will be renewed and receive its paradisiacal glory.

11. We claim the privilege of worshiping Almighty God according to the dictates of our own conscience, and allow all men the same privilege, let them worship how, where, or what they may.

12. We believe in being subject to kings, presidents, rulers, and magistrates, in obeying, honoring, and sustaining the law.

13. We believe in being honest, true, chaste, benevolent, virtuous, and in doing good to all men; indeed, we may say that
we follow the admonition of Paul—We believe all things, we
hope all things, we have endured many things, and hope to
be able to endure all things. If there is anything virtuous,
lovely, or of good report or praiseworthy, we seek after
these things.

The vision expressed in the Articles is consistent with an
Arminian/Methodist understanding of the fall of humanity and the
openness of salvation to all (articles 2-3). Smith was no Calvinist. As is
well known, the Mormon movement is part of a larger movement
known as Christian primitivism (article 6) though, of course, the LDS
Church claims to be "the one true Church".[12] The Articles also show a
strong charismatic emphasis (articles 5 and 7), in keeping with the worship style of the earliest LDS community. The charismatic element in
Mormon worship largely died out in the Church's first generation.[13]

Unlike the Protestant groups of his day, Smith believed in revelation beyond the Bible, not only with the Book of Mormon as Scripture
but with continuing revelation (articles 8-9). By 1842 the Saints had
already included Doctrine and Covenants as additional scripture.
Smith also moved beyond his Protestant roots in suggesting that
America plays a special part in the divine economy (article 10). This is
no surprise given the American focus in The Book of Mormon.

Contemporary Issues

Whatever Latter-day Saints share in common with traditional
Christians or with mainstream society has not exempted Mormons
from antagonism. This was especially true in the early decades of
Mormonism. Even today the LDS Church is the brunt of political and
social attack, shown in nasty critique on Romney while he was the
Republican candidate for President, in *South Park* satire, and in various
negative newspaper cartoons and editorials. The smash hit 2011 musical The Book of Mormon is a further example of attack on the LDS,
though the play suggests nothing sinister about Mormonism.[14] Most of
the deeper modern antipathy to Mormonism has to do with specific
theological critique by evangelical Christians and general scorn by
atheist and secular voices.

One internal drama in modern LDS history involved a case of forgery and murder. In October 1985 Salt Lake City was rocked by a series of bomb explosions that killed two people. Mark Hofmann, a dealer in rare Mormon documents, was charged with murder. He was found guilty and sentenced to life in prison. The case is important for students of Mormonism because of Hofmann's dealings with top Mormon leaders. The evidence suggests that the Mormon leaders were not open both about material in Church archives and about their full interaction with Hofmann. As well, some critics noted that the LDS prophet at the time failed to use his alleged supernatural gifts to detect Hofmann's forgeries.[15]

LDS leaders received enormous criticism for their resistance to the Equal Rights Amendment in the 1970s and early 1980s. Sonia Johnson was excommunicated from the Church in 1979 for her outspoken endorsement of the ERA.[16] A further round of unrest over feminism took place in the early 1990s, symbolized in the action taken against three leading LDS feminists Lavina Fielding Anderson, Maxine Hanks, and Lynne Kanavel-Whitesides. They were part of the September Six— six members who were either excommunicated or disfellowshipped in September 1993.[17] Since those times of unrest the LDS leaders have taken a more nuanced approach to feminism. This softening explains the return of Maxine Hanks to the Church in 2012 and the tolerance towards feminists in the LDS blogosphere.[18]

Gay rights continue to occupy a more contested space for LDS authorities, especially since the Church supported Proposition 8, a California ballot proposition in 2008 that sought to overturn recognition of same-sex marriage. LDS Church authorities backed Proposition 8 and many Mormons supported the campaign financially and in door-to-door canvassing. The Proposition was passed in November 2008 but eventually overturned by a California court in 2010. As of fall 2012 the case awaited appeal before the U.S. Supreme Court.

The LDS Church has consistently endorsed sexual practice only within traditional marriage bonds. However, rhetoric against homosexuality has softened in recent years. LDS leaders have also recognized that some of the therapies designed to "cure" gays have not been as successful as promised. The LDS Church is open to gays serving in Church positions as long as they do not violate Church teachings against homosexual behavior.[19] In 2011 Mitch Wayne, an openly gay LDS member, was chosen as executive secretary to the LDS Bishop in a part of San Francisco. Wayne has expressed willingness to obey Church law.[20] The pro-gay LDS group Affirmation, founded in 1977, believes Church leaders should bless same-sex marriage.[21]

The biggest challenge LDS authorities face today is the growth of dissent and skepticism within LDS circles. This has been noted most clearly by Marlin Jensen, the official LDS Church Historian and a member of the First Quorum of the Seventy. Jensen has acknowledged a growing attrition rate among members. Jensen also took part in what is known as the Swedish Rescue, a program which involved official LDS plans to reverse high apostasy rates among Mormons in Sweden.[22] The program is being applied to other countries where members are leaving the Church or experiencing loss of faith.

The Mormon Stories organization is attempting to explore doubts among contemporary Latter-day Saints through its Why Mormons Question project. The major figure in Mormon Stories is John Dehlin, a former LDS missionary who found himself increasingly uncertain about major elements of LDS doctrine. In spite of his reputation as a New Order Mormon, Dehlin decided in early 2013 to stick with the LDS Church, a move that led to sharp criticism by critics of Mormonism, particularly ex-members. Many traditional Mormons objected to Dehlin's skepticism and self-identification as a Mormon and he was targeted by some major Mormon apologists. Dehlin's life story is a powerful illustration of the powerful grip of Mormon culture.[23] The same holds true for Joanna Brooks, another Mormon Stories leader, and author of *The Book of Mormon Girl*.[24]

The Why Mormons Question project has already completed one major survey which charted the major reasons that lead to loss of belief. Of these, the top ten are:

1. Polygamy/polyandry
2. Doubts about authenticity of the Book of Abraham
3. Blacks and the Priesthood
4. DNA and the origins of the American Indian
5. Masonic influences in the temple ceremony
6. Multiple, conflicting versions of the First Vision

7. Anachronisms in the Book of Mormon
8. Women and the Priesthood
9. Past church positions on science, age of the earth, evolution, etc.
10. Issues with the authenticity or credibility of the priesthood restoration[25]

Of course, only a miniscule number of Latter-day Saints have lost belief when contrasted to the millions of Mormons who continue to believe, live and share the Mormon Gospel. With Romney's run for U.S. President creating a Mormon moment, LDS authorities continue to look for new ways to increase effectiveness in public, including social media. The "I am a Mormon" campaign has been hugely popular, as one example. As of 2012 the Church occupied the #1 ranking on Facebook for religious groups and charities.[26]

Joseph Smith
and the First Vision

The following assertion on a major LDS website reflects the conviction of millions of Mormons worldwide. "Joseph Smith's first vision stands today as the greatest event in world history since the birth, ministry, and resurrection of Jesus Christ. After centuries of darkness, the Lord opened the heavens to reveal His word and restore His Church through His chosen prophet."[1]

The First Vision is the cornerstone of LDS theology and can be traced directly to Joseph Smith himself. Here are his words from *The Pearl of Great Price,* one of the LDS scriptures:

> 5 Some time in the second year after our removal to Manchester, there was in the place where we lived an unusual excitement on the subject of religion.... 7 I was at this time in my fifteenth year.... 8 During this time of great excitement my mind was called up to serious reflection and great uneasiness.... 11 While I was laboring under the extreme difficulties caused by the contests of these parties of religionists, I was one day reading the Epistle of James, first chapter and fifth verse, which reads: *If any of you lack wisdom, let him ask of God, that giveth to all men liberally, and upbraideth not; and it shall be given him.* 14 So, in accordance with this, my determination to ask of God, I retired to the woods to make the attempt. It was on the morning of a beautiful clear day, early in the spring of eighteen hundred and twenty. 16 ... just at this moment of great alarm [attack by an evil spirit], I saw a pillar of light exactly over my head, above the brightness of the sun, which descended gradually until it fell upon me. 17 ... When the light rested upon me

I saw two Personages, whose brightness and glory defy all description, standing above me in the air. One of them spake unto me, calling me by name and said, pointing to the other— *This is My Beloved Son. Hear Him!* [18] ... I asked the Personages who stood above me in the light, which of all the sects was right (for at this time it had never entered into my heart that all were wrong)—and which I should join. [19] I was answered that I must join none of them, for they were all wrong; and the Personage who addressed me said that all their creeds were an abomination in his sight."[2]

This First Vision is of paramount significance in Mormon life. Besides being the centerpiece of LDS missionary witness, many Mormon artists have depicted the First Vision in their paintings, and LDS leaders have constantly affirmed the absolute importance of Smith's famous encounter. Gordon B. Hinckley, a recent LDS Prophet, wrote in 1998:

Our entire case as members of The Church of Jesus Christ of Latter-day Saints rests on the validity of this glorious First Vision.... Nothing on which we base our doctrine, nothing we teach, nothing we live by is of greater importance than this initial declaration. I submit that if Joseph Smith talked with God the Father and His Beloved Son, then all else of which he spoke is true. This is the hinge on which turns the gate that leads to the path of salvation and eternal life.[3]

In the 2007 PBS documentary on the Mormons, Hinckley had these words to say:

Well, it's either true or false. If it's false, we're engaged in a great fraud. If it's true, it's the most important thing in the world. Now, that's the whole picture. It is either right or wrong, true or false, fraudulent or true. And that's exactly where we stand, with a conviction in our hearts that it is true: that Joseph went into the Grove; that he saw the Father and the Son; that he talked with them; that Moroni came; that the Book of Mormon was translated from the plates; that the priesthood was restored by those who held it anciently. That's our claim.

That's where we stand, and that's where we fall, if we fall. But we don't. We just stand secure in that faith."[4]

Elder Carlos E. Asay wrote these emotionally rich words on the same topic:

A believing boy took one small step and prayed. A loving Father in Heaven listened and responded. What has resulted could rightfully be referred to as one giant leap for mankind. All the towers ever built and all the spaceships ever launched pale in comparison to Joseph Smith's first vision. Though men fly higher and higher into the heavens, they will not find God or see his face unless they humble themselves, pray, and heed the truths revealed through the Prophet of the Restoration (Joseph Smith).[5]

Imaginary Vision?

As LDS leaders note, the credibility of Joseph Smith's account of the First Vision determines Mormonism's integrity. However, Smith's dating of the vision to 1820 does not line up with the events he claims happened around the same time. He states that he sought God's help when a revival was going on in his area. That revival has been shown by Wesley P. Walters and others to have taken place in 1824, four years after Smith's date for the First Vision. There are no indications of a revival in his home area in 1820 in the church records and other historical documents Walters has used. This raises the question: Is it possible that Smith could forget the year of his face-to-face encounter with God the Father and Jesus Christ?[6]

Joseph Smith's famous First Vision account is contradicted by other accounts from him and from other Mormon leaders of his time. The official First Vision story comes from 1838, but two other accounts from Smith date from 1832 and 1835. These three accounts disagree on when the vision occurred, where it occurred, why it occurred, and who it was that appeared to Joseph.[7]

The discrepancies in his stories do not represent trivial matters or differences in detail that one expects in any multiple telling of the same event.[8] His various accounts and those by other Mormons differ on significant items like date, place, rationale, and the identity of his divine guests. The accounts have to be read in sequence or side by side for one to realize the extent to which the versions of the First Vision vary. In the 1838 account God the Father and Jesus announce that all churches are corrupt while in Smith's 1832 writing he claims to know this "by searching the Scriptures." In the 1832 version Smith has a vision of Jesus alone while the 1838 account mentions both Father and Son.

When Oliver Cowdery (assisted by the prophet) wrote the first history of Mormonism in 1834–1835, there is no mention at all of a visit from God the Father and/or the Son. Rather, the focus is on an angelic visitor. Further, this is dated to a revival in 1823 and the divine encounter takes place in Smith's room, not in the forest. The account reads in part:

> The stature of this personage was a little above the common size of men in this age; his garment was perfectly white, and had the appearance of being without seam. Though fear was banished from his heart, yet his surprise was no less when he heard him declare himself to be a messenger sent by commandment of the Lord, to deliver a special message, and to witness to him that his sins were forgiven, and that his prayers were heard.[9]

The following chart illustrates the discrepancies in the various reports about Smith's visions. The 1838 account is the one quoted in LDS Scripture.

Date of account	Account by?	Father and Son mentioned?	Repentance mentioned?	Revival mentioned?	Gold plates mentioned?
1827	Joseph Sr. and Joseph Jr. as told to Willard Chase	No	No	No	Spirit tells of gold plates
1827	Martin Harris as told to Rev. John Clark	No	No	No	Angel tells of gold plates
1830	Joseph Jr. as told to Peter Bauder	No	No	No	Angel tells of gold plates
1832	Joseph Jr. as written in History	Jesus only	Yes	No	Yes
1834-1835	Oliver Cowdery with Joseph Jr. in LDS periodical	No	Yes	Yes 1823	Yes
1835	Joseph Jr. to Joshua, a Jewish minister	No	No	No	No
1835	Joseph Jr. to Erastus Holmes	No	No	Yes 1820	Indirectly
1838	Joseph Jr. in Pearl of Great Price (official count)	Father and son	No	Yes 1820	Yes

Date of account	Account by?	Father and Son mentioned?	Repentance mentioned?	Revival mentioned?	Gold plates mentioned?
1844	Joseph Jr. for chapter in book by Daniel Rupp	No	No	No	No
1859	Martin Harris in Tiffany's Monthly	No	No	No	Yes

The earliest reports about Mormonism, from both friend and foe, make no mention of the 1820 First Vision. Martin Harris, one of the three witnesses to the Book of Mormon, does not talk about it at all during the 1820s and early 1830s. In 1827, Rev. John A. Clark, a pastor in Palmyra, spent time with Harris talking about Smith and his revelations. The whole focus from Harris was on the gold plates. Harris, one of the Three Witnesses to the Book of Mormon, said nothing at all about the 1820 encounter.[11]

This major point was made by Fawn Brodie in her *No Man Knows My History,* considered a classic biography of Joseph Smith. According to Brodie, because of written attacks, Smith's associates wrote rebuttals defending Smith. However none of those defenses mention the First Vision. Brodie wrote:

> No one...intimated that he had heard the story of the two gods. At least, no such intimation has survived in print or manuscript.... If something happened that spring morning in 1820, it passed totally unnoticed.... The awesome vision he described in later years may have been the elaboration of some half-remembered dream stimulated by the early revival excitement and reinforced by the rich folklore of visions circulating in his neighborhood. Or it may have been sheer invention, created some time after 1834 when the need arose for a magnificent tradition to cancel out the stories of his fortune-telling and money-digging.[12]

Other factors indicate that the official First Vision account is a later fabrication. For example, Joseph Smith kept little of his thinking to himself. He was not shy or introverted. His diaries, journals, and letters display a willingness to talk openly about key events in his life. During the 1820s he entertained his parents and siblings with accounts about American Indians. It is telling that he did not tell them of any divine visitation.[13] It is even more significant that his alleged visit from the Father and Son is absent from any private or public material from or about Smith while he was writing and publishing The Book and Mormon and founding the Mormon Church.

There are other key issues in the case against the integrity of the official First Vision account. If Smith knew directly from God the Father and the Son that all churches were an abomination back in 1820, why did he try to join the Methodist Church in 1828? The opposition of several Methodists to Smith scuttled his membership, but several primary witnesses recorded his interest in the Methodist cause.[14] As well, he did not warn his family members that all churches were wrong during the 1820s or settle the family squabbles over which church to attend by reference to what God the Father and Jesus said to him.

If he saw God and Jesus in 1820, why does Oliver Cowdery claim that in 1823 Smith prayed to learn "if a Supreme being did exist"?[15] Likewise, if Smith saw in 1820 that God the Father has a body, why did he not teach that truth from 1820 through 1838? For example, the original 1835 edition of Doctrine and Covenants, one of the LDS scriptures, claims that the Father is "a personage of spirit."[16]

The fact that early critics of Mormonism never mention the First Vision is significant. Even James B. Allen, a Mormon historian, recognizes this point:

> The earliest anti-Mormon literature attacked the Book of Mormon and the character of Joseph Smith but never mentioned the first vision. Alexander Campbell, who had some reason to be bitter against the Mormons because of the conversion of his colleague Sidney Rigdon in 1830, published one of the first denunciations of Joseph Smith in 1832. It was entitled Delusions: An Analysis of the Book of Mormon and contained no mention of the first vision. In 1834 E. D. Howe published

Mormonism Unvailed, which contained considerable damaging material against Joseph Smith...but again no mention of the first vision.[17]

The historical evidence against the traditional LDS account of the First Vision in 1820 is overwhelming, but the Saints are trained from early on in their spiritual life to answer objective concerns about history with a subjective testimony of what they feel to be true.[18] Over the years Mormon leadership has not presented a thorough discussion of the topic to the worldwide Mormon community though LDS scholars examine the issue in limited academic contexts. LDS leaders sometimes suppressed relevant historical documents related to historicity and the First Vision but the Internet now offers open access on these and other issues.[19]

There is a larger theological issue at stake in assessing the First Vision. It has to do with the nature of the Church and the integrity of the promise of Jesus about the Church. In Matthew 16:18 Jesus states: "I will build my church; and the gates of hell shall not prevail against it" (KJV)., Given this promise, there is something very disturbing about an alleged message in 1820 that all churches on earth are an abomination. This is especially true in light of the fact that that LDS members are taught that the gospel disappeared from the earth shortly after the New Testament age and was not restored for eighteen centuries. That is a grim and false view of the Christian gospel and the Church that Jesus built.[20]

The claim of total apostasy rings especially hollow in light of the fact that the original Mormon gospel amounts to nothing more than a modified Protestantism. The only startling differences have to do with the addition of a new prophet and one extra Scripture. However, even the theology of The Book of Mormon is not that far removed from major Protestant perspectives on the Christian faith. The Articles of Faith do not break much ground from standard Methodist leanings of the day, as noted in the preceding chapter. Of course, the claim of total apostasy added to Smith's allure as the one chosen by God to restore the gospel.

In the last few years Mormon scholars are writing in softer tones about the exclusivist and nasty language in the 1820 vision.[21] If the newer, gentler understanding is the correct one, then Mormon leaders should apologize for the condemning language often used by Mormon prophets and scholars in times past. Brigham Young accused the "so-called Christian world" of "groveling in darkness." John Taylor, the third prophet, said Christianity "is a perfect pack of nonsense." Apostle Orson Pratt noted that "all other churches are entirely destitute of all authority from God."[22]

In spite of a softer reading of the First Vision, there is no convincing evidence that God and Jesus visited Joseph Smith in 1820. The 1838 version of that vision was created by Smith to buttress his authority during a time when his leadership was being contested. Mormon scholars try to explain away the contradictions between the various accounts noted earlier. Regardless of that endeavor, the silence of a First Vision account from 1820 through the start of the church in 1830 is absolutely deafening.

The Prophet
and Buried Treasure

On July 28, 1971 Wesley Walters, a scholar of Mormon origins, made a breathtaking discovery while searching for historical material in the basement of the County Jail in Norwich, New York, southeast of Syracuse. Much to his astonishment he found two documents that implicated Joseph Smith in criminal activity. One document was the bill of Justice Albert Neely for various trial costs. The bill contains these words: "Joseph Smith The Glass Looker March 20, 1826 Misdemeanor To my fees in examination of the above cause 2.68."[1] The term "Glass Looker" was used for those who used psychic means to find buried treasure. It was also known as money digging.[2]

The other document Walters discovered was the bill from a Constable Philip De Zeng for guarding a prisoner named Joseph Smith. De Zeng charged $1.25 for "Serving Warrant on Joseph Smith & travel" and $1.75 for "Attendance with Prisoner two days and 1 night" and another $1.00 for "20 miles travel" with Smith. He also charged another small amount for the subpoenaing of "12 witnesses and travel."[3]

From today's perspective the small financial costs involved in the 1826 trial make the court case sound insignificant. However, the case has enormous importance. Walters' discovery of the court material created shock waves among Mormon scholars. Walters was subject to intense criticism by various LDS writers. There were even arguments that Walters may have tampered with the documents.[4] However, most Mormon scholars now recognize that the documents Walters brought to light are genuine. His 1971 discovery led to major shifts in the Mormon reaction to claims that Joseph Smith had a criminal past.[5]

The issue of Smith's alleged glass looking or money digging came up regularly during the early days of Mormonism. The topic failed to gain much traction after Mormons moved West under Brigham Young. Things changed, however, with the publication of Fawn Brodie's *No Man Knows My History*. Hers was the first major critical biography of the prophet. Brodie included an account of Smith's 1826 trial that appeared in Fraser's Magazine in 1873. Here is part of that magazine account:

STATE OF NEW YORK v. JOSEPH SMITH
Warrant issued upon written complaint upon oath of Peter G. Bridgeman, who informed that one Joseph Smith of Bainbridge was a disorderly person and an imposter. Prisoner brought before Court March 20, 1826.

Prisoner examined: says that he came from the town of Palmyra, and had been at the house of Josiah Stowel in Bainbridge most of time since; had small part of time been employed by said Stowel on his farm, and going to school. That he had a certain stone which he had occasionally looked at to determine where hidden treasures in the bowels of the earth were; that he professed to tell in this manner where gold mines were a distance underground, and had looked for Mr. Stowel several times, and had informed him where he could find these treasures, and Mr. Stowel had been engaged in digging for them.[6]

Brodie's accusations about money digging and the report from the 1873 magazine were dismissed as false by key Mormon writers. Francis W. Kirkham, an influential LDS writer on the Book of Mormon, denied the reality of the court case but did recognize the implications of the allegations.

If any evidence had been in existence that Joseph Smith had used a seer stone for fraud and deception, and especially had he made this confession in a court of law as early as 1826, or four years before the Book of Mormon was printed, and this confession was in a court record, it would have been impossible for him to have organized the restored Church.[7]

Hugh Nibley, one of the most famous LDS scholars, made a similar admission. He wrote in his book *The Myth Makers* that "...if this court record is authentic it is the most damning evidence in existence against Joseph Smith." It would, he wrote, amount to "the most devastating blow to Smith ever delivered."[8]

Since Nibley's day Mormon academics have learned to live with the authenticity of the court records and the fact that the founder of Mormonism engaged in money digging.[9] It is surprising that Kirkham and Nibley were so dogmatic on the issue since they both knew about evidence that pointed to Smith's involvement in money digging, whether or not there was a court case about it. Public writings about Smith's glass looking and trial appeared as early as 1831. One report states:

Messrs. Editors— ... thinking that a fuller history of their founder, Joseph Smith, jr., might be interesting ... I will take the trouble to make a few remarks.... For several years preceding the appearance of his book, he was about the country in the character of a glass-looker: pretending, by means of a certain stone, or glass, which he put in a hat, to be able to discover lost goods, hidden treasures, mines of gold and silver, &c.... In this town, a wealthy farmer, named Josiah Stowell, together with others, spent large sums of money in digging for hidden money, which this Smith pretended he could see, and told them where to dig; but they never found their treasure. At length the public, becoming wearied with the base imposition which he was palming upon the credulity of the ignorant, for the purpose of sponging his living from their earnings, had him arrested as a disorderly person, tried and condemned before a court of Justice..... This was four or five years ago.[10]

In reference to Smith's legal troubles, Oliver Cowdery, one of the Three Witnesses to The Book of Mormon, proclaimed that the prophet was "honorably acquitted."[11] Dan Vogel has shown how that view is "indefensible."[12] While the evidence suggests a guilty verdict, this is not the main issue that Mormons must face. Dale Morgan notes: "From the point of view of Mormon history, it is immaterial what the finding of the court was on the technical charge of being 'a disorderly person and an imposter'; what is important is the evidence adduced, and its bearing on the life of Joseph Smith before he announced his claim to be a prophet of God.[13]

Proof of Smith's money digging comes from his own father-in-law Isaac Hale. As mentioned earlier, Smith married Isaac's daughter Emma in 1827, against the wishes of her father. One of Hale's chief objections to Joseph had to do with his practice of money digging. Hale wrote:

> I first became acquainted with Joseph Smith, Jr. in November, 1825. He was at that time in the employ of a set of men who were called 'money diggers;' and his occupation was that of seeing, or pretending to see by means of a stone placed in his hat, and his hat closed over his face. In this way he pretended to discover minerals and hidden treasure.... young Smith... asked my consent to his marrying my daughter Emma. This I refused, and gave him my reasons for so doing; some of which were, that he was a stranger, and followed a business that I could not approve;... while I was absent from home [he] carried off my daughter...[14]

There is an interesting parallel to Hale's account in an affidavit from Peter Ingersoll, dated December 2, 1833 in Palmyra, New York. Ingersoll claims that he was hired by Joseph to move some of Emma's furniture from her dad's house to Manchester, New York.

> When we arrived at Mr. Hale's, in Harmony, Pa. from which place he had taken his wife, a scene presented itself, truly affecting. His father-in-law (Mr. Hale) addressed Joseph, in a flood of tears: "You have stolen my daughter and married her. I had much rather have followed her to her grave. You spend your time in digging for money—pretend to see in a stone, and thus try to deceive people." Joseph wept, and acknowledged he could not see in a stone now, nor never could; and that his former pretensions in that respect, were all false. He then promised to give up his old habits of digging for money and looking into stones.[15]

The Prophet and Buried Treasure

It was common knowledge in the Palmyra area that Joseph Jr. and his father frequently engaged in money digging. Rev. John Clark made this derogatory remark about the Smith family in general and Joseph in particular.

> They lived a sort of vagrant life, and were principally known as money-diggers. Jo from a boy appeared dull and utterly destitute of genius; but his father claimed for him a sort of second sight, a power to look into the depths of the earth, and discover where its precious treasures were hid. Consequently long before the idea of a GOLDEN BIBLE entered their minds, in their excursions for money-digging, which I believe usually occurred in the night, that they might conceal from others the knowledge of the place where they struck upon treasures, Jo used to be usually their guide, putting into a hat a peculiar stone he had through which he looked to decide where they should begin to dig.[16]

Early critics of Mormonism collected testimonies about the Smith family involvement in money digging. Witnesses targeted Joseph Sr., Joseph Jr. and two of Joseph's brothers. However, Joseph Jr. was the main one under attack given his claim to divine revelation and leadership of the one true church. In the 1830s there is a grudging admission by Joseph that he had engaged in searching for buried treasure. However, Smith understates the frequency of his involvement and downplays the superstitious, magical elements.

The magical element in Smith's life is now recognized by scholars of Mormon history. It should also be recognized that early Mormons had a gullible side to their faith. One example of this involves a story Brigham Young, the second Mormon prophet, told in later years:

> I will take the liberty to tell you of another circumstance...Oliver Cowdery went with the Prophet Joseph when he deposited these plates....the angel instructed him to carry them back to the hill Cumorah, which he did. Oliver says when Oliver and Joseph went there, the hill opened, and they walked into a cave, in which there was a large and spacious room....They laid the plates on a table; it was a large table that stood in the room. Under this table there was a pile of plates as

much as two feet high, and there were altogether in this room more plates than probably many wagon loads...[17]

Of course, early Mormon belief in the supernatural did not usually include respect for the practice of money digging. After all, most traditional Christians and Mormons in the 1830s (and now) would regard the psychic hunt for treasure as part of the occult or dark side. The money digging in the Smith family could take on some rather sordid realities, as noted by William Stafford, a neighbor:

> Old Joseph and one of the boys came to me one day, and said that Joseph Jr. had discovered some very remarkable and valuable treasures, which could be procured only in one way. That way, was as follows: That a black sheep should be taken on to the ground where the treasures were concealed—that after cutting its throat, it should be led around a circle while bleeding. This being done, the wrath of the evil spirit would be appeased: the treasures could then be obtained, and my share of them was to be four fold. To gratify my curiosity, I let them have a large fat sheep. They afterwards informed me, that the sheep was killed pursuant to commandment; but as there was some mistake in the process, it did not have the desired effect.[18]

Joseph Smith engaged in money digging from 1823 through sometime in 1826. Apart from the intrinsic problems with the practice itself, there are disturbing implications related to his integrity. First, Smith's money digging was carried on during the time period when he was supposedly preparing to receive the golden plates of The Book of Mormon. Given this, we have a strange juxtaposition of undisputed criminal activity with alleged divine visitations.

It is disturbing that Mormon leaders today do not worry at all that their prophet was a lawbreaker. In a rather pathetic apologetic, Richard Bushman even claims that magic was a "preparatory gospel" that paved the way for Joseph's work in translating the gold plates.[19]

What Bushman knows but fails to really deal with is that Joseph Smith did not really drop his psychic ways. When he translated the golden plates he continued to use the same seer stone that he employed in money digging. Because LDS leaders do not usually make use of the seer-stone part of the standard account of Smith translating the Book of Mormon, few Mormons know of the translation's disreputable origins.[20]

Testimonies that Smith used the seer stone in his translation work are abundant. Smith's father-in-law Isaac Hale wrote: "The manner in which he [Joseph] pretended to read and interpret, was the same as when he looked for the 'money diggers,' with the stone in his hat, and his hat over his face, while the book of plates was at the same time hid in the woods."[21]

As strange as it may seem, The Book of Mormon was birthed via an occult practice, one that earned Mormonism's founding prophet a criminal sentence. This is not a very inspiring start to a group that claims to be the only true Church of Jesus Christ.

Those Many Wives

Many people still associate the LDS Church with polygamy even though engaging in polygamy or plural marriage will result in excommunication from the Church of Jesus Christ of Latter-day Saints. Polygamy was once part of mainstream Mormonism. Brigham Young, the second Mormon prophet, led the church into open proclamation and practice of plural marriage after settling in Utah in 1847. He had fifty-five wives. It wasn't until 1890 that the LDS presidency issued a manifesto against polygamy.[1]

Mormon polygamy originated in the life of Joseph Smith. However, LDS leaders did not publicly admit to the practice of polygamy during Smith's life, realizing that details about the prophet and plural marriage would prove problematic to LDS members and the non-Mormon public.[2] Regardless, plural marriage remains an integral part of the history of the prophet, with effects felt throughout Mormon history.

There is now no doubt that Joseph Smith, in spite of his public denials, engaged in plural marriage. There is extended debate about when the practice began, the exact number of plural wives, whether the plural marriages involved sex, and so forth; however, evidence shows Smith to be a polygamist.[3] Debate about the origins of polygamy often turns to the case of Fanny Alger, who lived with Joseph and Emma during the 1830s. Rumors circulated in the Mormon community that Joseph was in love with her. More significant, Oliver Cowdery, one of Joseph's closest friends, accused the prophet of an affair with Fanny. Here is how Fawn Brodie, one of the most famous biographers of Smith, captured the matter:

Sometime in 1835 it began to be whispered about that [Smith] had seduced a 17-year-old orphan girl whom Emma had taken into the family....Whether or not Fannie Alger bore Joseph a child, it was clear that the breath of the scandal was hot upon his neck.... Oliver Cowdery knew the report of an illicit affair between the girl and the prophet to be true, for they 'were spied upon and found together.' Cowdery made no secret of his indignation and Joseph finally called him in and accused him of perpetuating the scandal.... [I]n a letter from Oliver Cowdery to his brother Warren A. Cowdery, dated Far West, Missouri, 21 January 1839] Oliver wrote: 'We had some conversation in which in every instance I did not fail to affirm that what I had said was strictly true. A dirty, nasty, filthy affair of his and Fanny Alger's was talked over in which I strictly declared that I had never deserted from the truth in that matter and as I supposed was admitted by himself.' ... Cowdery himself stoutly refused to exonerate the prophet and eventually was excommunicated from the Church for several misdemeanors, among them 'insinuating that the prophet had been guilty of adultery.'[4]

Smith never answered publicly for the Alger episode. Emma reportedly drove Fanny from her home after seeing Fanny and Joseph in a compromising situation in their barn. A few early witnesses suggested that Fanny had a child, but there is no record of a child from any relationship with Smith. Fanny's departure from the Smith household happened in either 1835 or 1836. She left town and later married, but never provided details about her relationship with Smith.

Mormon scholars have usually either denied the affair or explained it as the first plural marriage of the Mormon prophet. There is some indication that Fanny may have been secretly married to Joseph in 1833, a position adopted by Todd Compton in his study *In Sacred Loneliness.*[5] However, George D. Smith, another historian of polygamy, does not include Fanny on the list of polygamist wives, nor does Fawn Brodie. Beyond the Alger case, there is some evidence for a plural marriage of Joseph with Lucinda Pendleton Morgan Harris in 1838. Her name is in Andrew Jenson's 1887 list of plural wives.[6] What makes this case significant is that Lucinda's marriage to the prophet comes a full three years before Smith makes plural marriage a regular, though secret, occurrence. On April 5, 1841, he married Louisa Beaman, often called the first plural wife. On October 27, 1841, Smith married Zina Diantha Huntington, and he was married to Presendia Lathrop Huntington the same year on December 11. The number of plural marriages increased dramatically in 1842 and 1843.[7] Compton contends that Smith's last plural marriage took place on November 2, 1843, to a woman named Fanny Young. For Compton, this adds up to thirty-three wives.[8] Fawn Brodie argued for forty-eight in her *No Man Knows My History*.

Throughout his life Joseph Smith never attempted to defend polygamy publicly, either to his mass Mormon following or to non-Mormons. In fact, Joseph claimed publicly that he advocated monogamy and that accusations of polygamy were false. However, he justified it privately to some Mormon leaders and to the women he sought to wed. He said that God wanted him to restore the practice that was given to Old Testament saints like Abraham, David, and Solomon. Smith claimed that plural marriage was part of the restoration of the gospel.[9]

Most Mormons are truly unaware of the turmoil and heartache connected with Smith's polygamous ways. Consider his only legal wife Emma. She married Smith in 1827, choosing Joseph over the wishes of her parents. She stuck with him through the Mormon journeys to Ohio, Missouri, and Illinois, enduring persecution, all the while remaining committed to her marriage vows. She must have been angry when she saw or heard the first signs of her husband's infidelity. Imagine her astonishment when she was told of divine wrath if she opposed plural marriage. Verse 54 of Section 132 of Doctrine and Covenants is probably one of the saddest and most striking verses in Mormon scripture. Of plural wives, it reads: "But if she [Emma] will not abide this commandment she shall be destroyed." William Clayton, a top Mormon leader and confidant, wrote in his diary that Smith took "harsh measures" against Emma. This probably related to her constantly complaining about his redesign of their wedding vows.

In advancing polygamy Smith rejected several commands in the Book of Mormon against polygamy (Jacob 1:15; 2:23–27; 3:5; Mosiah 11:2–4, 14; Ether 10:5). Smith also used various tactics to obtain plural wives and to maintain secrecy. Nine months after his secret marriage to Sarah Ann Whitney, Smith performed a mock public wedding for Sarah and Joseph C. Kingsbury so that fellow Mormons would never suspect his liaison with Sarah.

Smith threatened women with damnation if they resisted his proposal of marriage. He would also threaten that a woman's family would be destroyed if a plural marriage was denied. Smith told one of his wives that their relationship had been established in their prior existence.[10] He told Zina D. Huntington that he (Joseph) would be destroyed if she did not consent.[11] Smith would also get Mormon women open to polygamy to pressure other Mormon women to adopt the practice. Further, he would arrange for a husband or brother to be sent on a mission trip to remove any resistance they might have to his new polygamy partner.

Smith pressured Mormons to publicly deny that polygamy was practiced, and he instead accused others of polygamy.[12] In August 1842 he sent 380 Mormon elders across the nation to do damage control on allegations of polygamy. He even pressured various Mormons to swear out affidavits denying that polygamy was part of Mormon life. Thus, Smith suborned perjury, a criminal act. Two of the signatures were from plural wives Smith had already married.

Smith married single women, already married women, and widows. He married sisters (for example, Maria Lawrence and her sister Sarah from Pickering, Ontario) and even a mother and daughter. He married younger teenagers (Helen Mar Kimball was fourteen when she wed) and older women, though most of his brides were in their twenties and thirties.

Many of Joseph's wives believed, of course, that polygamy was God's will. This belief applied to whole families at times. For example, Sarah Ann Whitney's parents both accepted polygamy and encouraged their daughter's marital relationship with Joseph. A letter to them and Sarah Whitney (whom he married on July 27, 1842) is interesting. It was written two months after their wedding ceremony. Joseph was in hiding over legal troubles. Part of his letter reads:

> My feelings are so strong for you since what has passed lately
> between us ... it seems, as if I could not live long in this way;
> and if you three would come and see me ... it would afford me

great relief … I know it is the will of God that you should comfort me now in this time of affliction … the only thing to be
careful of; is to find out when Emma comes then you cannot be
safe, but when she is not here, there is the most perfect safety
… burn this letter as soon as you read it; keep all locked up in
your breasts … you will pardon me for my earnestness on this
subject when you consider how lonesome I must be.[13]

There is a rather ironic side to the vows that Sarah's father, Newel,
read over Sarah Ann and Joseph on their wedding day: "You both
mutually agree to be each other's companion so long as you both shall
live, preserving yourselves for each other and from all others and also
throughout all eternity."[14] Smith had married Eliza Snow the prior
month. Martha McBride would be his new bride in August, and there
would be at least eighteen other brides in 1843. Some Mormon women
resisted and denounced Smith's advances.. One of the most famous
cases involves Nancy Rigdon, the daughter of Sidney Rigdon, an
important convert to Mormonism. When Nancy Rigdon refused his
advances and her father stood by her, rumors spread that Nancy was a
prostitute.[15] Like Nancy Rigdon, most LDS female members today have
a deep aversion to polygamy though a lone female voice or two speak
with admiration about Smith's polygamous ways. One female blogger
posted on "Why I Would Totally Have Slept with Joseph Smith."[16]

Other Mormon leaders besides Rigdon were also opposed to
polygamy. Joseph Smith's own brother Don Carlos was one of them. He
is reported to have said: "Any man who will teach and practice the doctrine of spiritual wifery will go to hell; I don't care if it is my brother
Joseph."[17] William Law, formerly a right-hand man to the prophet,
broke with Smith over plural wives. In early June 1844, he printed
details about Mormon polygamy in the one and only issue of his newspaper *The Nauvoo Expositor*.[18] Joseph Smith spearheaded the destruction of the printing press on June 10, which led to a public outcry.
Smith was subsequently arrested and jailed in Carthage, Illinois on
June 25, 1844. Two days later an angry mob stormed the jail and the
prophet and his brother Hyrum were killed in a shoot-out.

While this brought the prophet's life to an end, the practice of
polygamy continued among the LDS for another half century. Under
pressure from the US government the LDS prophet Wilford Woodruff

issued a manifesto against polygamy in 1890. This did not stop the practice completely and major LDS leaders performed plural marriages in spite of public statements to the contrary. Increased social and political pressure on the LDS Church led to a second manifesto in 1904.[19] This time the ban was strongly enforced and the LDS Church was no longer a safe place for polygamists. After 1904 those in favor of plural marriage started their own groups and claimed to stand true to the path of their founding prophet Joseph Smith.[20]

As one would expect, the current Mormon leadership are not providing the Mormon faithful with much detail of Smith's polygamous ways. Discovery that Smith broke three of the Ten Commandments in his schemes to arrange his plural marriages (thou shall not lie, thou shall not steal, and thou shall not commit adultery) is one of the top reasons why Mormons are abandoning the Mormon Church. Many of them now call Joseph Smith, the founding prophet of the LDS, a sexual predator.[21]

Even if that term is not used, some clear facts remain about Joseph Smith's actions in relation to polygamy. He lied about it. He told others to lie about it. He used his prophetic office to pressure women into marrying him. He took the Lord's name in vein as he made his moves on the various women. He even claimed an angel threatened his life if he did not engage in plural marriage. He broke his own wedding vows through his polygamous actions. He married women who were already married thus leading them to commit adultery. He married women under the normal age for marriage for that time period in American history. He threatened those who resisted his plans in relation to polygamy.

The issue with Joseph Smith is not about polygamy per se or whether polygamy is ever right. It is about the lying, stealing, adultery, manipulation, coercion, spousal abuse and criminal behavior that Joseph engaged in while he practiced his particular brand of polygamy. It is about a so-called prophet of God using his alleged divine mantle to bed young women, including two under his own guardianship. Mormons who can defend all this can defend anything.

Name	Marriage date	Age	Marital status
Emma Hale (Smith)	Jan 17, 1827	22	N/A
1. Fanny Alger	Early 1833	16	Single
2. Lucinda Pendleton Morgan Harris	Est. 1838	37	Married
3. Louisa Beaman	Apr. 5, 1841	26	Single
4. Zina Diantha Huntington (Jacobs)	Oct. 27, 1841	20	Married
5. Presendia Lathrop Hungtington (Buell)	Dec. 11, 1841	31	Married
6. Agnes Moulton Coolbirth	Jan. 6, 1842	31	Single
7. Sylvia Porter Sessions Lyon	Feb. 8, 1842	23	Married
8. Mary Elizabeth Rollins Lightner	Jan. 17, 1842	23	Married
9. Patty Bartlett (Sessions)	Mar. 9, 1842	47	Married
10. Marinda Nancy Johnson (Hyde)	Apr. 1842	27	Married
11. Elizabeth Davis (Brackenbury Dufee)	Bef. Jun. 1842	50	Married
12. Sarah Maryetta Kingsley (Howe Cleveland)	Bef. Jun. 29, 1842	53	Married
13. Delcena Johnson (Sherman)	Bef. Jul. 1842	37	Single
14. Eliza Roxcy Snow	Jun. 29, 1842	38	Single
15. Sarah Ann Whitney	Jul. 27, 1842	17	Single
16. Martha McBride (Knight)	Aug. 1842	37	Single
17. Ruth D. Vose (Sayers)	Feb. 1843	34	Married
18. Flora Ann Woodworth	Spring 1843	16	Single
19. Emily Dow Partridge	Mar. 4, 1843	19	Single
20. Eliza Maria Partridge	Mar. 8, 1843	22	Single
21. Almera Woodward Johnson	Apr. 1843	30	Single
22. Lucy Walker	May 1, 1843	17	Single
23. Sarah Lawrence	May 1843	17	Single

Name	Marriage date	Age	Marital status
24. Maria Lawrence	May 1843	19	Single
25. Helen Mar Kimball	May 1843	14	Single
26. Hannah Ells	1843	29	Single
27. Elvira Annie Cowles (Holmes)	Jun. 1, 1843	29	Married
28. Rhoda Richards	Jun. 12, 1843	58	Single
29. Desdemona Fullmer	Jul. 1843	32	Single
30. Olive Grey Frost	Summer 1843	27	Single
31. Melissa Lott	Sep. 20, 1843	19	Single
32. Nancy Mariah Winchester	1842 or 1843	14	Single
33. Fanny Young (Murray)	Nov. 2, 1843	56	Single

The Church
and the Prophets

All the major choices in religion eventually rest on questions of authority. Which sources are regarded as sacred? What person or persons have a final say on what constitutes truth? Can religious leaders make mistakes and be forgiven for them? Is there just one true church? Do certain creeds have binding power over doctrine? Can past teachings be overturned?

The LDS approach to authority is multifaceted. Beyond the proclaimed submission to God, the LDS Church grants authority to the prophetic work of Joseph Smith and to the four scriptures related to his ministry. These are the Bible (including his own inspired translation), the Book of Mormon, Doctrine and Covenants, and the Pearl of Great Price.[1] From Smith's revelations and the teaching of the Scriptures, LDS members confidently believe that God has restored the LDS Church as "the one true Church" on earth.

The LDS Church beliefs are that its present authority on earth is vested in a modern-day prophet. The current prophet is Thomas Monson. He and his two counselors form the First Presidency, and they are joined by a Quorum of Twelve Apostles.[2] These fifteen leaders form the highest human authority in the Church, with the First Presidency and its prophet at the top. Under their authority are eight Quoroms of "Seventy" men who provide leadership as well. The worldwide work of the Mormon Church is then shared with other LDS faithful, both men and women. Several major organizations are led by women, most notably the Primary (dealing with the education of children) and Relief Society, founded in 1842, and the principle support group for women.[3]

The prophet of the Mormon Church occupies a position similar to the Pope in the Roman Catholic Church. While the Mormon prophet typically does not claim infallibility, his authority is rarely challenged and his word is usually final and binding. While Mormon prophets regularly consult with other leaders, they are not required to. Highly revered by the LDS faithful, the prophet is trusted to lead the church, and is believed to act under the direct guidance of God.

Prophets of the Mormon Church

1. Joseph Smith (1805–44)

2. Brigham Young (1801–77)

Sustained as Prophet: 1847

3. John Taylor (1808–87)

Sustained as Prophet: 1880

4. Wilford Woodruff (1807–98)

Sustained as Prophet: 1889

5. Lorenzo Snow 1814–1901

Sustained as Prophet: 1898

6. Joseph F. Smith (1838–1916)

Sustained as Prophet: 1901

7. Heber J. Grant (1856–1945)

Sustained as Prophet: 1919

8. George Albert Smith (1870–1951)

Sustained as Prophet: 1945

9. David O. McKay (1873–1970)

Sustained as Prophet: 1951

10. Joseph Fielding Smith (1876–1972)

Sustained as Prophet: 1970

11. Harold B. Lee (1899–1973)

Sustained as Prophet: 1972

12. Spencer W. Kimball (1895–1985)

Sustained as Prophet: 1973

13. Ezra Taft Benson (1899–1994)

Sustained as Prophet: 1985

14. Howard W. Hunter (1907–95)

Sustained as Prophet: 1994

15. Gordon B. Hinckley (1910–2007)

Sustained as Prophet: 1995

16. Thomas Monson (1927–)

Sustained as Prophet: 2008

The prophet and the priesthood

Mormons trace the authority vested in their prophets to Joseph Smith, their first prophet. He was both prophet and priest. The restoration of the priesthood is one of the most important aspects of LDS ecclesiology since the LDS expressly denies the validity of any other religious groups. LDS Prophet Spencer Kimball claimed "there is no priesthood anywhere else today than in this restored [LDS] Church."[4] Mormonism teaches that for churches to act without this authority is a grievous sin. Kimball stated: "Presumptuous and blasphemous are they who purport to baptize, bless, marry, or perform other sacraments in the name of the Lord while in fact lacking his specific authorization." This is a stark declaration that there is no real authority outside of the Church of Jesus Christ of Latter-day Saints.

Within Mormonism, there are currently two priesthoods, the Aaronic and a greater one known as the Melchizedek priesthood. Smith claimed to have received both priesthoods. The first is said to have been restored on May 15, 1829, when John the Baptist granted the Aaronic priesthood to Joseph Smith and Oliver Cowdery. Section 13 of Doctrine and Covenants records the conferral:

> Upon you my fellow servants, in the name of Messiah I confer the Priesthood of Aaron, which holds the keys of the ministering of angels, and of the gospel of repentance, and of baptism by immersion for the remission of sins; and this shall never be taken again from the earth, until the sons of Levi do offer again an offering unto the Lord in righteousness.[5]

Mormons believe that the Melchizedek priesthood was given by Peter, James, and John to Smith and Cowdery by early 1830.[6]

The Mormon claim of priesthood restoration is straightforward on the surface; however, relevant revelations about the priesthood were altered. Joseph Smith rewrote documents to try and show that the priesthood began before the Mormon Church was founded. The first revelations on the priesthood were written in the 1833 Book of Commandments, but the material was changed when given in the Doctrine and Covenants in 1835. This changing of Mormon revelation has been documented by Grant Palmer, Michael Quinn, Jerald and Sandra Tanner, Dan Vogel, and Michael Marquardt, among others.[7] The latter notes: "Missionaries in the early church before 1835 did not claim they held priesthood authority that was restored by the ancient apostles Peter, James and John."[8] The chart below has the original revelation and then its altered form.

Book of Commandments 1833	Doctrine and Covenants 1835
28:6 Behold this is wisdom in me, wherefore marvel not, for the hour cometh that I will drink of the fruit of the vine with you, on the earth, and with all those whom my Father hath given me out of the world:	**Behold, this is wisdom in me; wherefore, marvel not, for the hour cometh that I will drink of the fruit of the vine with you on the earth, and with** Moroni, whom I have sent unto you to reveal the Book of Mormon, containing the fulness of my everlasting gospel, to whom I have committed the keys of the record of the stick of Ephraim; 27:6 And also with Elias, to whom I have committed the keys of bringing to pass the restoration of all things spoken by the mouth of all the holy prophets since the world began, concerning the last days; 27:7 And also John the son of Zacharias, which Zacharias he (Elias) visited and gave promise that he should have a son, and his name should be John, and he should be filled with the spirit of Elias; 27:8 Which John I have sent unto you, my servants, Joseph Smith, Jun., and Oliver Cowdery, to ordain you unto the first priesthood which you have received, that you might be called and ordained even as Aaron; 27:9 And also Elijah, unto whom I have committed the keys of the power of turning the hearts of the

Book of Commandments 1833...cont.	Doctrine and Covenants 1835...cont.
	fathers to the children, and the hearts of the children to the fathers, that the whole earth may not be smitten with a curse; 27:10 And also with Joseph and Jacob, and Isaac, and Abraham, your fathers, by whom the promises remain; 27:11 And also with Michael, or Adam, the father of all, the prince of all, the ancient of days; 27:12 And also with Peter, and James, and John, whom I have sent unto you, by whom I have ordained you and confirmed you to be apostles, and especial witnesses of my name, and bear the keys of your ministry and of the same things which I revealed unto them; 27:13 Unto whom I have committed the keys of my kingdom, and a dispensation of the gospel for the last times; and for the fulness of times, in the which I will gather together in one all things, both which are in heaven, and which are on earth; 27:14 And also with all those whom my Father hath given me out of the world.

David Whitmer, one of the Three Witnesses to the Book of Mormon, offered a possible explanation for the changes between the documents. He argued that Sidney Rigdon (another prominent Mormon) influenced Smith to start a priesthood. So, relevant words were inserted into earlier revelations so that priesthood authority looks like it goes back to the start of the LDS Church. Whitmer wrote:

Authority is the word we used for the first two years in the church—until Sidney Rigdon's days in Ohio. This matter of two orders of priesthood in the Church of Christ, and lineal priesthood of the old law being in the church, all originated in the mind of Sydney Rigdon.... This is the way the High Priests and the "priesthood" as you have it, was introduced into the Church of Christ almost two years after its beginning—and after we had baptized and confirmed about two thousand souls into the church."[30]

Earlier in his book, Whitmer made this charge (emphasis in original):

You have *changed the revelations* from the way they were first given and as they are today in the Book of Commandments, to support the error of Brother Joseph in taking upon himself the office of Seer to the church. You have *changed the revelations to support the error of high priests.* You have changed the revelations to support the error of a President of the high priesthood, high counselors, etc. You have *altered the revelations* to support you in going beyond the plain teachings of Christ in the new covenant part of the Book of Mormon.[10]

Even if Whitmer is wrong about the Rigdon influence, there is no doubt that revelations changed. Historian LaMar Petersen, writing in 1957, notes (emphasis in original):

More than four hundred words were added to this revelation of August 1829 in Section 27 of the *Doctrine and Covenants,* the additions made to include the names of heavenly visitors and two separate ordinations. The *Book of Commandments* gives the duties of Elders, Priests, Teachers, and Deacons and refers to Joseph's apostolic calling but there is no mention of Melchizedek Priesthood, High Priesthood, Seventies, High Priests, nor High Councilors.[11]

The conscious alteration of revelations related to the priesthood gives reason to reject Smith's claims to priesthood authority. Smith, however, suffered no doubts. He said: "Truth is Mormonism. God is the author of it."[12]

Questions also have to be raised about who is the legitimate heir to Smith's prophetic mantle. At the time of his death there were several claimants, including a son and other Mormon leaders. To Mormons the "inner testimony" by LDS members certifies for them that Brother Monson is now the prophet of the church and that the Church of Jesus Christ of Latter-day Saints is the only true Church. However, this subjective rationalization fails to address whether or not Brigham Young was the rightful successor to Smith. What if Smith wanted his mantle to pass to his son or brother or to Rigdon or Strang or another prominent Mormon of the time?

The Authority of the Prophet

How the LDS are supposed to regard their prophet was answered in a famous lecture on 14 Fundamentals by Ezra Taft Benson. Benson gave his lecture at Brigham Young University on February 26, 1980, five years before he was sustained as prophet of the church. The authority and power he asserted for the role were startling.

14 Fundamentals

First: The prophet is the only man who speaks for the Lord in everything.

Second: The living prophet is more vital to us than the standard works.

Third: The living prophet is more important to us than a dead prophet.

Fourth: The prophet will never lead the Church astray.

Fifth: The prophet is not required to have any particular earthly training or credentials to speak on any subject or act on any matter at any time.

Sixth: The prophet does not have to say "Thus saith the Lord" to give us scripture.

Seventh: The prophet tells us what we need to know, not always what we want to know.

Eighth: The prophet is not limited by men's reasoning.

Ninth: The prophet can receive revelation on any matter, temporal or spiritual.

Tenth: The prophet may be involved in civic matters.

Eleventh: The two groups who have the greatest difficulty in following the prophet are the proud who are learned and the proud who are rich.

Twelfth: The prophet will not necessarily be popular with the world or the worldly.

Thirteenth: The prophet and his counselors make up the First Presidency—the highest quorum in the Church.

Fourteenth: The prophet and the presidency—the living prophet and the First Presidency—follow them and be blessed; reject them and suffer.

When Benson spoke in his lecture about the current prophet being more important than scripture, he referenced a Mormon Church meeting from the 1830s.

Brother Brigham took the stand, and he took the Bible, and laid it down; he took the Book of Mormon, and laid it down; and he took the Book of Doctrine and Covenants, and laid it down before him, and he said: 'There is the written word of God to us, concerning the work of God from the beginning of the world, almost, to our day. And now,' said he, 'when compared with the living oracles those books are nothing to me; those books do not convey the word of God direct to us now, as do the words of a Prophet or a man bearing the Holy Priesthood in our day and generation. I would rather have the living oracles than all the writing in the books.' That was the course he pursued. When he was through, Brother Joseph said to the congregation; 'Brother Brigham has told you the word of the Lord, and he has told you the truth.'[13]

Benson's adulation of the Mormon prophet's importance undermines the authority of the Bible and the other standard Mormon works. Thus, the promotion of the prophet's status comes at the expense of scripture itself, a stunning reality. Though the speech alarmed some LDS leaders, it is presented without disclaimer on the official website of the church.[14] It is deeply disturbing that Benson could contend that "the living prophet is more vital to us than the standard works" and not be instantly and publicly corrected by other LDS authorities and by the LDS public.

Likewise, the assertion that the "living prophet will never lead the Church astray" is an alarming affront to to plain facts. LDS history shows clearly that various prophets led Mormons into what was later declared as false teaching. For example, Brigham Young, the second LDS prophet, taught three doctrines that LDS authorities now consider heresy.

First, he preached a theory of "blood atonement" where certain sins can only be covered by the shedding of the guilty person's blood.[15]

Second, he advanced the theory that Adam was really God on earth. This is known as the Adam-God doctrine and was formally repudiated by later LDS prophet Spencer Kimball.[16] Third, Young's sermons and writings advanced a racist ideology toward blacks.[17] These are major errors from a prophet of the Mormon Church. The last one in particular has had an enormous negative impact that still remains on the LDS Church. Brigham Young is proof that one cannot explicitly trust the words of a Mormon prophet. Further, his racist theories were advanced, at least implicitly, by every Mormon prophet from Young until Kimball's major revision of policy in 1978.

Underlying these various points about prophetic failure in LDS history is a more important concern that involves the very heart of LDS church life. The vast majority of LDS members adopt an uncritical, naïve and irrational trust in the LDS prophet, the first presidency, and the other General Authorities of the Church. This has been a constant and sad reality in LDS history, illustrated by blind obedience to Joseph Smith, Brigham Young, and other prophets. The enormous adulation of the leadership leads to a church body unable to even name error, mistake, coverup, and sin among the Brethren. This explains the unblinking agreement to whatever the leaders want at General Conferences. This mentality leads, of course, to the crackdown on dissenters and the silencing of wisdom's voice when leaders err.

On a practical level, the dictatorial powers of the First Presidency afford little room for authentic criticism by the LDS majority. Most LDS members do not really know what is going on at the top of their own church. Further, even if they knew, dissent is seldom appreciated, even if on target. Consider one current reality in recent LDS Church life. The current Mormon prophet is becoming increasingly mentally incapacitated. In the near future, he will no longer be able to do many of the functions associated with his office. It is troubling that most Mormons do not even know this fact about their own prophet and even more troubling that the LDS system allows little chance of correction in the way prophets are chosen.

Distinct Mormon Churches [defunct and current]

• Aaronic Order

• Apostolic United Brethren

- Center Branch of the Lord's Remnant
- Christ's Church
- Church of Christ (David Clark)
- Church of Christ at Halley's Bluff
- Church of Christ (Fetting/Bronson)
- Church of Christ (Restored)
- Church of Christ (Temple Lot)
- Church of Christ with the Elijah Message (Rogers)
- Church of Christ "With the Elijah Message," established anew in 1929
- Church of Jesus Christ (Bickertonite)
- Church of Jesus Christ (Bulla)
- Church of Jesus Christ (Cutlerite)
- Church of Jesus Christ (Drew)
- Church of Jesus Christ of Latter-day Saints (majority group)
- Church of Jesus Christ of Latter-day Saints (Strangite)
- Church of Jesus Christ of the Saints in Zion
- Church of Jesus Christ (Toney)
- Church of Jesus Christ (Zion's Branch)
- Church of the First Born of the Fullness of Times
- Church of the New Covenant in Christ
- Churches of Christ in Zion
- Confederate Nations of Israel
- Holy Church of Jesus Christ
- Independent Church of Jesus Christ of Latter-day Saints
- Millennial Church of Jesus Christ
- Community of Christ (formerly Reorganized Church of Jesus Christ of Latter Day Saints)
- Restoration Branches Movement
- Restored Church of Jesus Christ (Walton)

The Church and the Prophets

- Restoration Church of Jesus Christ of Latter-day Saints
- School of the Prophets
- School of the Prophets (Wood)
- True Church of Jesus Christ Restored
- United Order Effort
- Zion's Order, Inc.

The Book of Mormon

The importance of the Book of Mormon to the Latter-day Saints and other Mormon groups cannot be overstated. The book was a key part of the original interest people had in Joseph Smith and the church he founded in 1830 and is the central scriptural text now used by LDS missionaries all over the world. The LDS belief in the centrality of the Book of Mormon is stated on an official LDS website:

> God chose Joseph as a prophet, seer, revelator and translator to restore The Church of Jesus Christ in modern time, and the Book of Mormon was essential to this restoration. Joseph Smith was given an extraordinary calling, and because he kept himself worthy of the blessings of heaven, he was able to bring the Book of Mormon to the world."[1]

History of the Book of Mormon

According to Joseph Smith, an angel revealed gold plates buried in the hill Cumorah, four miles south of Palmyra, New York on September 22, 1823, and on the same date in 1827, the angel allowed him to take the plates. These are the plates Mormons believe form the basis of "another testament of Jesus Christ"—the Book of Mormon.

Smith said the plates contained the records of three ancient Jewish groups who migrated to the Americas before the time of Christ. According to Smith, he returned the golden plates to the angel after the Book of Mormon was completed

Smith and the earliest Mormons claimed that he could translate the plates through revelation even if the plates were not with him in the same room. He would usually look at a seer stone, a psychic tool, and "see" the translation of the reformed Egyptian material on the plates reflected in the stone.

The main story of the Book of Mormon surrounds Lehi, an Israelite prophet who brought his family to the Americas in 600 BC (1 Nephi 18). The story recounts how Nephi and Laman, two sons of Lehi, became bitter enemies, how their descendants fought for centuries, how the Nephites were destroyed in AD 421, and finally how Moroni, a survivor of the last battle, buried the records of his family in Cumorah.

Two other family groups get brief attention in the Book of Mormon: the Jaredites and the Mulekites. The book of Ether tells the story of the Jaredites who supposedly came to the Americas around 2200 BC and died off about two centuries before Christ was born. The book of Omni recounts the story of the Mulekites, descendants of Mulek, the sole surviving son of King Zedekiah who was the last king of Judah in the book of Kings. Although Zedekiah is mentioned in the Bible, Mulek is not. According to the book of Omni, the Mulekites arrived in the Americas in 586 BC. The family merged with the Nephites three centuries later.

In a similar way to how the books of the Old Testament present family histories, tribal histories, and national histories of the Israelites, the histories of the Nephites, Mulekites, and Jaredites dominate the Book of Mormon. The documents describe ancient cities, wars, the changing shape of government, civil law, literacy (especially among the Nephites), economic details, and more. However, the overriding concern behind the events portrayed in the Book of Mormon is the spiritual history of the tribes as they either obeyed or rebelled against God.

The central point of the Book of Mormon involves its testimony to Jesus Christ. Elder Russell Nelson of the Quorum of the Twelve Apostles notes this: "Study of the Book of Mormon is most rewarding when one focuses on its *primary* purpose—to testify of Jesus Christ."[2] This involves not only predictions about his first incarnation but the announcement of his appearance in the Americas after his resurrection. An entry on Jesus in *The Encyclopedia of Mormonism* states:

> About 30 B.C. a group of Lamanites were converted to Christ when God's light shone and his voice spoke out of an enveloping cloud of darkness (Helaman. 5:33–43). Twenty-five years later, a prophet named Samuel the Lamanite foretold that

more significant signs of light would appear at the time of Jesus' birth and that massive destruction and darkness would be seen at his death (Helaman 14:2–27). Five years after Samuel, Nephi[3] heard the voice of Jesus declaring that he would come into the world "on the morrow," and the signs of Jesus' birth were seen; thirty-three years and four days after that, all the land heard the voice of Christ speaking through the thick darkness on the Western Hemisphere that accompanied his crucifixion and death (3 Nephi 9). Within that same year, they saw the resurrected Jesus Christ come down out of heaven (3 Nephi 11:8). The resurrected Christ appeared to a congregation of righteous Nephites at their temple and allowed them to feel the wounds in his hands and feet, and thrust their hands into his side (3 Nephi. 11:15). They heard the voice of the Father saying, "Behold my Beloved Son, in whom I am well pleased, in whom I have glorified my name-hear ye him" (3 Nephi 11:7). For three days, Jesus was with these people. He called and ordained twelve disciples, and taught his gospel of faith, repentance, baptism, and the gift of the Holy Ghost.... He healed their sick, and in the presence of angels and witnesses he blessed the parents and their children.[3]

Historicity and the Book of Mormon

The vast majority of LDS believe that the reports about the three families in The Book of Mormon are historical. Likewise, most Mormons believe that prophecies of Jesus in the Book of Mormon and his ministry to the Nephite people are equally historical. Joseph Smith claimed that the Book of Mormon is "the most correct of any book on Earth."[4] Mormon apologists have produced an enormous literature defending the historical truth of the central Mormon text.[5]

The question of historical authenticity is somewhat distinct from whether or not the doctrinal teaching of the Book of Mormon is true. The latter does not depend on the former. The Book of Mormon teaches one God (monotheism), God is Father, Son, and Spirit, God is eternal, and salvation is by grace through trust in the atonement of Christ. This point about the doctrine of the Book of Mormon is important, especially since Joseph Smith departs from some of its major teachings later in his life, as we will see.[6]

The historical question itself is simple. Either the events in the Book of Mormon happened or they didn't. The choice either to believe or disbelieve the historicity of the Book of Mormon is based on radically opposing sets of assumptions and historical claims.

The traditional Mormon view is that Joseph Smith presented facts: he found the plates of the Book of Mormon, which outline real events that affected ancient Jews who came to the Americas and lived their lives just as the Mormon scripture states. That would include details that there really was a city named Zarahemla (Helaman 1: 18), a "sword of Laban" was actually brought to the New World as told in 1 Nephi, an Ammon was a servant to King Lamoni (Alma 17:25), and there was a last Jaredite named Coriantumr (Omni 1:21). It would also mean that Jesus did come to the Americas after his resurrection (see 3 Nephi) and that Moroni really hid his history books in the hill Cumorah, are also accurate.

The defense of the Book of Mormon stands on four assumptions firmly held by LDS believers: Joseph Smith told the truth, only divine inspiration could be behind the Book of Mormon, the Book of Mormon is a fulfillment of biblical prophecy, and witnesses saw golden plates and testified to their reality.

First, Mormons implicitly trust Smith's integrity, similar, in some senses, to their trust in Jesus. What non-Mormons must note is how difficult it is for most Mormons to entertain the possibility that Joseph Smith might have embellished the truth or lied. To ask a Mormon to question Smith's integrity would be like asking a Jew to question the teachings of Moses, a traditional Christian to question Jesus or Paul, or a Muslim to question Muhammad.[7] This high trust of Joseph Smith is shown in the frequent declarations in LDS writers that salvation hinges on recognizing his role in the restored gospel.

Second, Mormons argue that it would be impossible for a rather uneducated young man like Joseph Smith to have produced such a work by his mid-twenties. They conclude that Smith's explanation of supernatural aid is the most satisfactory view of the origins of the sacred text.[8]

Third, Mormons also claim there are biblical passages predicting the arrival of the Book of Mormon. The most common biblical passage cited is from Ezekiel 37:15–17:

Again the word of the Lord came to me, saying, "As for you, son of man, take a stick for yourself and write on it: 'For Judah and for the children of Israel, his companions.' Then take another stick and write on it, 'For Joseph, the stick of Ephraim, and *for* all the house of Israel, his companions.' Then join them one to another for yourself into one stick, and they will become one in your hand. (NKJV)

Mormons believe that this passage refers to the union of the Bible plus the Book of Mormon, so to them, the Book of Mormon fulfills Ezekiel's prophecy.

Fourth, Mormons often seek to prove the truth of the Book of Mormon by relying on the accounts of the "Three Witnesses" and the "Eight Witnesses," who said they saw the golden plates with their own eyes and testified to the divine authorship of Smith's most famous translation. Most attention here is given to the "Three Witnesses" who were Oliver Cowdery, David Whitmer, and Martin Harris, who provided funding for publication of the Book of Mormon.

There are insurmountable problems with the four traditional Mormon assumptions regarding the validity of the Book of Mormon.

First, Joseph Smith's integrity should be questioned at the outset. This can be show from many angles.

As we noted earlier, his practice of polygamy involved lying, coercion, adultery, and criminality. Likewise, as we also noted, he was involved in criminal and dishonest money-digging schemes. Further, in the 1830s multiple charges of fraud were lodged against Smith after he reportedly received a revelation to found a Kirtland, Ohio bank, which failed miserably, resulting in heavy financial losses to investors. Smith might be the only person in history to start an Anti-banking company, a move done after the Ohio legislature refused to incorporate Smith's new financial institution.[9]

Smith's ego should also be a matter of concern. There is, of course, debate about whether he really translated gold plates for the Book of Mormon. There is also debate about his translation ability in relation to the Book of Abraham, as we shall see later. However, Smith's pronouncements about brass plates from Kinderhook, Illinois turned out to be bogus. Smith was fooled by a group of local hoaxers.[10]

Smith also illustrated his egocentric ways by unalloyed dogmatism on matters that should strike anyone as beyond his competence. His translation of the Bible, for example, often bears no relation to the actual ancient texts of Scripture. His rendition of John 1:1 can be seen as ignorant by any first year student of Greek. Only Mormons entertain the notion that John 1:1 should be translated: "In the beginning was the *gospel preached through the Son. And the gospel was the word, and the word was with the Son, and the Son was with God, and the Son was of God.* "[11]

His bombastic comments in sermons fail to hide his lack of learning. John Kessler, a scholar of Hebrew and my colleague, said that Smith "misreads the Hebrew syntax" in his 1844 sermon in the grove.[12] Likewise, Smith's pronouncement that the Garden of Eden was in Missouri shows an astounding lack of knowledge and humility that cannot be defended by referencing divine revelation. The same holds true when he so casually pronounced on the identity of a body discovered in Pike County, Illinois on June 3, 1834. That Joseph could comment on the man's name (Zelph) and history (a Lamanite who served under a leader named Onandagus) is a tribute both to his audacity and the credulity of his followers.[13]

Further, Joseph's narcissism is evident in his run for U.S. President in 1844. One can only imagine what a full time media would have discovered on polygamy, his polytheistic teachings, his money digging, the financial exploits in Kirtland, his provocations in Missouri, the secret Temple ceremonies with their Masonic roots, and his handling of those who dared question him.

Joseph's ego is also revealed in his pontificating about the future, a facet of his ministry that led to numerous false statements and false prophecies. For example, Smith was wrong in his predictions about finding treasure in Salem, about Mormons settling in Missouri, about people living on the moon and about the end of the world.[14] He is also one of the few divines in history to note his superiority over Jesus. Here is what he stated near the end of his life:

Come on! ye prosecutors! ye false swearers! All hell, boil over! Ye burning mountains, roll down your lava! for I will come out on top at last. I have more to boast of than ever any man had. I am the only man that has ever been able to keep a whole church together since the days of Adam. A large majority of the whole have stood by me. Neither Paul, John, Peter, nor Jesus ever did it. I boast that no man ever did such a work as I. The followers of Jesus ran away from Him; but the Latter-day Saints never ran away from me yet...When they can get rid of me, the devil will also go.[15]

It would help on-going evangelical-Mormon dialogue to have LDS authorities speak clearly against the outrageous claim that Joseph Smith did more than Jesus Christ. They should also address his false prophecies, criminal behavior, immoral treatment of women, and bogus Bible translations. In regard to the Book of Mormon itself, there is much lacking in the testimonies of the witnesses. Consider the Three Witnesses: Cowdery, Whitmer, and Harris. Their witness to the golden plates usually involved a visionary experience, not a case of physical sight. All three left Smith at one time or another. Most important, they could provide no details about the writing on the plates, and the plates disappeared from history.[16] The easiest explanation for the absence of the gold plates is that they did not exist. On this, it is singularly significant that Smith would cover up the alleged gold plates with a cloth and warn people not to look under the cloth. Were the gold plates radioactive on sight?

Second, associating the Ezekiel passage with the Book of Mormon is questionable since the context in Ezekiel is the unification of the twelve tribes of Israel under a Davidic king. Ezekiel 37:18–28 explains that the sticks are the tribes from the northern and southern kingdoms reunited in the land given to the children of Jacob.

Third, the Book of Mormon itself is replete with evidence that it is a product of the nineteenth century and not of Jewish tribes living more than a thousand years prior to the founding of the United States. It deals with religious issues common to Smith's Day. The anachronism was noted by the book's earliest critics, with the most famous quote in this regard from Church of Christ preacher Alexander Campbell:

This prophet Smith, through his stone spectacles, wrote on the plates of Nephi, in his book of Mormon, every error and almost every truth discussed in New York for the last ten years. He decides all the great controversies—infant baptism, ordination, the trinity, regeneration, repentance, justification, the fall of man, the atonement, transubstantiation, fasting, penance, church government, religious experience, the call to the ministry, the general resurrection, eternal punishment, who may baptize, and even the question of freemasonry, republican government, and the rights of man.[17]

On these issues, the Book of Mormon usually adopted stances consistent with Joseph's Protestant background. The book opposes infant baptism (Moroni 8:10-22), uses Trinitarian language (1 Nephi 12:18, 2 Nephi 31:21) , affirms the need for new birth and repentance (2 Nephi 31:17), accepts Christ's atoning death (Jacob 4:11), and defends against the kind of agnosticism that arose after the Enlightenment. On the latter, see the dialogue with Korihor in Alma 30.

Contrary to popular Mormon sentiment, no archaeological or anthropological evidence exists for the Book of Mormon's version of events in the Americas from 2200 BC through AD 400.[18] Archaeologists do not use the Book of Mormon as a historical source when they interpret artifacts and ancient ruins. For example, the Smithsonian Institution in Washington has sent out notices in the past that The Book of Mormon is not used by its workers.[19] The National Geographic Society has also stated their researchers do not use the Book of Mormon as a scientific guide.[20] Likewise, anthropologists repudiate the common Mormon view that American Natives are descendants of ancient Jews who migrated to the Western hemisphere.

Here is the text of the form letter the Smithsonian Institution sent from 1996-1998:

THE DEPARTMENT OF ANTHROPOLOGY
SMITHSONIAN INSTITUTION

STATEMENT REGARDING THE BOOK OF MORMON

1. The Smithsonian Institution has never used the Book of Mormon in any way as a scientific guide. Smithsonian archaeologists see no direct connection between the archaeology of the New World and the subject matter of the book.

2. The physical type of the American Indian is basically Mongoloid, being most closely related to that of the peoples of eastern, central, and northeastern Asia. Archaeological evidence

indicates that the ancestors of the present Indians came into the New World—probably over a land bridge known to have existed in the Bering Strait region during the last Ice Age—in a continuing series of small migrations beginning from about 25,000 to 30,000 years ago.

3. Present evidence indicates that the first people to reach this continent from the East were the Norsemen, who briefly visited the northeastern part of North America around 1000 A.D. and then settled in Greenland. There is no evidence to show that they reached Mexico or Central America.

4. None of the principal Old World domesticated food plants or animals (except the dog) occurred in the New World in pre-Columbian times. This is one of the main lines of evidence supporting the scientific premise that contacts with Old World civilizations, if they occurred, were of very little significance for the development of American Indian civilizations. American Indians had no wheat, barley, oats, millet, rice, cattle, pigs, chickens, horses, donkeys, or camels before 1492. (Camels and horses were in the Americas, along with the bison, mammoth, and mastodon, but all these animals became extinct around 10,000 B.C. at the time the early big game hunters traveled across the Americas.)

5. Iron, steel, glass, and silk were not used in the New World before 1492 (except for occasional use of unsmelted meteroic iron). Native copper was worked in various locations in pre-Columbian times, but true metallurgy was limited to southern Mexico and the Andean region, where its occurrence in late prehistoric times involved gold, silver, copper, and their alloys, but not iron.

6. There is a possibility that the spread of cultural traits across the Pacific to Mesoamerica and the northwestern coast of South America began several hundred years before the Christian era. However, any such inter-hemispheric contacts appear to have been the results of accidental voyages originating in eastern and southern Asia. It is by no means certain that even such contacts occurred with the ancient

Egyptians, Hebrews, or other peoples of Western Asia and the Near East.

7. No reputable Egyptologist or other specialist on Old World archeology, and no expert on New World prehistory, has discovered or confirmed any relationship between archeological remains in Mexico and archeological remains in Egypt.

8. Reports of findings of ancient Egyptian, Hebrew, and other Old World writings in the New World in pre-Columbian contexts have frequently appeared in newspapers, magazines and sensational books. None of these claims has stood up to examination by reputable scholars. No inscriptions using Old World forms of writing have been shown to have occurred in any part of the Americas before 1492 except for a few Norse rune stones which have been found in Greenland.

9. There are copies of the Book of Mormon in the library of the National Museum of Natural History, Smithsonian Institution.[21]

Thomas Ferguson, a well-known LDS researcher, lost faith in the Book of Mormon when his archaeological digs failed to unearth any evidence of a Lamanite or Nephite world. A parallel crisis has developed over failure of Native American DNA to show any trace of Jewish roots. This is explored in Simon Southerton's ground-breaking work, *Losing a Lost Tribe*.[22] This failure at the genetic level has led to Mormon scholars scrambling to redefine the longstanding LDS views on the locale of the Book of Mormon. Difficulties here led to a change in the language about the Lamanites. Earlier editions of the Introduction to the Book of Mormon noted that the Lamanites "are the principal ancestors of the American Indians." The latest version of the Introduction states that they "are among the ancestors of the American Indians."[23]

The 2007 PBS documentary, *The Mormons,* included an interview with Michael Coe, professor emeritus of anthropology at Yale, who makes the claim that the Book of Mormon has no merit as a record of the Americas. Coe is one of the most famous experts on Central American history and culture. In an earlier and well-known article in *Dialogue,* he said, "The bare facts of the matter are that nothing, absolutely nothing, has ever shown up in any New World excavation which would suggest to a dispassionate observer that the Book of Mormon, as claimed by Joseph Smith, is a historical document relating to the history of early migrants to our hemisphere."[24]

Fifth, and very significantly, the Book of Mormon copies the King James Version of the Bible (1611), even down to the latter's use of italics. The Book of Mormon even includes some of the textual errors that were made in the King James Version.[25] For example, following Matthew 6:13 the Book of Mormon adds the long doxology to the Lord's Prayer, contrary to the earliest manuscripts of the New Testament. Some who have left the Mormon faith cite the exact parallels between the Book of Mormon text and the King James Version as a reason for departure from the church. One study notes that the Book of Mormon contains twenty-six full chapters from a 1769 edition of the King James Bible.[26] Why does the Book of Mormon allegedly from the fifth century A.D. quote the Bible in the words of a version over one thousand years later?

Finally, historians have tracked down other books that influenced Smith as he wrote the Book of Mormon. Of particular importance here is the work *View of the Hebrews* written by Ethan Smith and published in New York in 1823. Many of the concepts of the Book of Mormon duplicate Ethan Smith's earlier publication. In fact, former Mormon historian B. H. Roberts found the possible connections between *View of the Hebrews* and The Book of Mormon very troubling.[27] The factors above have created a crisis among some Mormons over the historicity of the Book of Mormon. It is another major reason why people are leaving the Mormon Church. Others are choosing to adopt a more liberal and even secular form of Mormonism, based on love of Mormon family and culture, while abandoning the literal truths of its most famous book. Of course, for most LDS members the Book of Mormon remains "another testament of Jesus Christ" and the greatest proof that Joseph Smith is a prophet of God. For the Mormon faithful the Book of Mormon is a clear sign that God has continued the process of revelation. There are other Scriptures to consider beyond the Book of Mormon. We will examine one such scripture in the next chapter.

Doctrine and Covenants

Before the Book of Mormon was published in the spring of 1830 Joseph Smith claimed he received revelations distinct from the angelic visitations related to the golden plates. Smith said these additional revelations began in 1828 and 1829, and that beginning in 1830 they increased in frequency. He reported new revelations until his death in 1844. These revelations form the main body of the Mormon sacred text known as *Doctrine and Covenants*. First published in 1835, the collection was revised as new revelations were received.

The introduction states:

> These sacred revelations were received in answer to prayer, in times of need, and came out of real-life situations involving real people. The Prophet and his associates sought for divine guidance, and these revelations certify that they received it. In the revelations one sees the restoration and unfolding of the gospel of Jesus Christ and the ushering in of the dispensation of the fullness of times. The westward movement of the Church from New York and Pennsylvania to Ohio, to Missouri, to Illinois, and finally to the Great Basin of western America and the mighty struggles of the Saints in attempting to build Zion on the earth in modern times are also shown forth in these revelations.[1]

The current edition contains 138 sections, mostly revelations from Smith, and a few from other LDS leaders. For example, section 136 provides a divine message to Brigham Young while section 138 involves a revelation to the sixth president of the church, Joseph F. Smith (the son of Joseph Smith's brother, Hyrum). Like many churches, sometimes official positions are revised over time. Two notable changes to LDS doctrine deal with polygamy and who can hold the office of priest. The first involves the issue of the Manifesto against Polygamy (1890), a ruling that runs against the famous revelation in section 132 that provides divine justification for plural marriage. The second official declaration presents the 1978 revelation to LDS President Spencer W. Kimball allowing blacks to hold the priesthood. The latter represents the most significant change in modern LDS history.

The LDS faithful believe that, along with the three other standard works (the Bible, Book of Mormon, and Pearl of Great Price), Doctrine and Covenants is the word of God. Beyond questions of divine authority, the material in Doctrine and Covenants provides important data when tracing the origins of the Book of Mormon, the founding of the Mormon Church, and the ongoing life in the first Mormon communities in New York, Ohio, Missouri, and Illinois.

Contents

C. Max Caldwell, a LDS scholar, has a useful outline of the contents of Doctrine and Covenants in *The Encyclopedia of Mormonism*.[2]

- Section 1 is the preface to the whole work and cites authorization from God to publish the revelations to Joseph Smith.

- Sections 2–9 focus on the book of Mormon and the importance of early Mormon leaders, including Joseph's father, in spreading the work of God.

- Sections 13, 18, 20, and 27 deal with the authority of the priesthood while section 19 focuses on the importance of the atonement of Christ.

- Sections 20–40 provide revelation during 1830, which was the first year of the church.

- Various doctrinal issues are dealt with including baptism (22), the sacrament of communion (27), and the Holy Spirit (29, 30, and 34, for example).

- Sections 35 and 37 deal with Joseph Smith's translation of the Bible.

- Members are directed to move to Ohio to establish Zion (37).

The longest section of Doctrine and Covenants, sections 41 through 123, reports on the church during its stay in Ohio and Missouri (1831–1939). Major revelations are given on morality (42, 58–59), labor (42, 60, 68, 75), dealing with the sick (42, 46, 63), how to handle transgressors (42, 58, 102, 107), importance of marriage/family (49), and discernment of counterfeit and evil (43, 46, 50, 52). The final major sections, 124–35, provide revelation in the last five years of the prophet's life. They instruct the faithful on the new Temple in Nauvoo (124) and about ordinances for the dead (124, 127–128). As well, section 107 gives instruction on the Quorum of the Twelve Apostles and that of the Seventy. There is also important revelation on the Godhead (130) and plural marriage (132).

Bill McKeever has noted the unique LDS teachings that derive from the Doctrine and Covenants.[3] The list includes the following:

- There is only one true church
- Those from other churches must be re-baptized
- The second coming will take place in Missouri
- The Garden of Eden was in Missouri
- Baptism for the dead is to be performed
- The Word of Wisdom forbids caffeine drinks, alcohol, and tobacco
- Celestial marriage is required to attain the highest heaven.

Changing Revelations?

Various Mormon leaders through history have made strong claims about the integrity of the revelations in Doctrine and Covenants. Apostle John A. Widtsoe said of them, "There has been no tampering with God's word."[4] President Joseph Fielding Smith declared that "each new revelation on doctrine and priesthood fitted in its place perfectly to complete the whole structure, as it had been prepared by the Master Builder."[5] One of the clearest statements about the care taken in transcribing divine revelation comes from Apostle Parley P. Pratt and is recorded in a footnote on page 173 of volume 1 of the *History of the Church*:

Each sentence was uttered slowly and very distinctly, and with a pause between each, sufficiently long for it to be recorded by an ordinary writer in long hand. This was the manner in which all his [Joseph] written revelations were dictated and written. There was never any hesitation, reviewing, or reading back, in order to keep the run of the subject; neither did any of these communications undergo revisions, interlinings or corrections. As he dictated them so they stood, so far as I have witnessed.

Nevertheless, both early and modern critics of Mormonism have noted that changes were made to what Smith and others claimed was divine revelation. One issue concerns "The Lectures on Faith," teachings given by Joseph Smith and others in 1834–1835. These lectures were included in every edition of Doctrine and Covenants from 1835 until 1921. For eighty-six years Mormons received the Lectures as part of sacred scripture and then the lectures were removed.

The removal of the Lectures on Faith is not comparable to a denomination making a change in its policies: The Lectures on Faith was viewed by Mormons as part of the word of God and its removal is more comparable to aa denomination deleting a book from the New Testament. In the LDS case, the Lectures on Faith had become problematic for church leaders because it affirms that God is a Spirit, contrary to the later teaching of Joseph Smith that God the Father has a body.[6]

Other serious complaints about changes in divine revelation involve alterations made between 1833 and 1835. The revelations to Joseph Smith were first recorded in the Book of Commandments in 1833 and later printed in 1835 under the current title Doctrine and Covenants. Some Mormon leaders immediately recognized that when the divine messages were released in the new 1835 volume, changes had been made. One of the earliest critiques came from David Whitmer, one of the Three Witnesses to the Book of Mormon. Although he did not abandon belief in the Book of Mormon, he eventually left the Mormon Church, stunned by changes made to the original revelations in the Book of Commandments. Near the end of his life he wrote:

Some of the revelations as they now appear in the Book of Doctrine and Covenants have been changed and added to. Some of the changes being of the greatest importance as the meaning is entirely changed on some very important matters; *as if the Lord had changed his mind* a few years after he gave the revelations.... Joseph and the church received it as being printed correctly. This I know. But in the winter of 1834 they saw that some of the revelations in the Book of Commandments had to be changed.[7]

Whitmer gives examples of the dramatic changes. He comments that a March 1829 revelation states that Smith was to be given no other gift than the task of translating the golden plates. The Book of Commandments reads "and he has a gift to translate the book, and *I have commanded him that he shall pretend to no other gift, for I will grant him no other gift*" (4:2).

Jerald and Sandra Tanner note the following in relation to Whitmer's concern:

By the year 1835, when this revelation was reprinted in the *Doctrine and Covenants,* Joseph Smith had pretended to at least one other gift besides that of translating the *Book of Mormon.* He had pretended to the gift of correcting the Bible (his so-called *Inspired Version*), and a short time after this he brought forth the Book of Abraham. Certainly this revelation commanding Joseph Smith to pretend to no other gift but to translate the *Book of Mormon* could not remain in its original form. The church had decided to go beyond the *Book of Mormon* and accept Joseph Smith's other writings as Scripture. This change in church policy necessitated a change in the revelation. Therefore, it was changed to read as follows: "And you have a gift to translate the plates; and this is *the first gift that I bestowed upon you*; and I commanded that you should pretend to no other gift, *until my purpose is fulfilled in this*; for I will grant unto you no other gift until it is finished" (*Doctrine and Covenants,* 5:4).[8]

David Whitmer also accused Smith of pasting in new instructions on the priesthood when he redid the relevant revelation in Doctrine and Covenants. He notes: "As if God had made a mistake in the first organization of the church, and left out these high important offices which are all above an elder; and as if God had made a mistake and left these high offices out of that revelation when it was first given. Oh the weakness and blindness of man!"[9] He added: "The majority of the members—poor weak souls—thought that anything Brother Joseph would do, must be all right; so in their blindness of heart, trusting in an arm of flesh, they looked over it and were led into error."[10]

The changes noted above and many others have been documented over the past forty years, especially by Jerald and Sandra Tanner, well-known critics of Mormonism.[11] Sandra, the great-great-granddaughter of Brigham Young, second LDS prophet, and Jerald left the LDS because of what they believed to be serious historical and theological errors in Mormonism.[12] Various teachings of Brigham Young were questioned by the Tanners, for example, Young's Blood Atonement, the notion that some sins can only be covered by the person's own blood being spilled.[13]

The Tanners have provided extensive data on the changes between the two versions of Mormon texts, Book of Commandments and Doctrine and Covenants.[14] They have also documented the resistance of LDS leaders to admitting that there were changes and to allowing the examination of relevant material. The Tanners wrote:

> For many years the Mormon leaders tried to suppress the *Book of Commandments*. They would not allow us to obtain photo-copies of the book from Brigham Young University. Fortunately, however, we were able to obtain a microfilm of the copy at Yale University and had the *Book of Commandments* printed by photo-offset.[15]

Michael Quinn, historian of Mormonism and former professor at Brigham Young University, mentioned the changes in Doctrine and Covenants and disturbing alterations of other Mormon material in a 1981 lecture "On Being a Mormon Historian."[16] Quinn also noted the resistance of LDS Church authorities to free enquiry and argued that "there have been occasions when LDS church leaders, teachers, and writers have not told the truth they knew about difficulties of the Mormon past but have offered to the Saints a mixture of platitudes, half-truths, omissions, and plausible denials."[17] Quinn was excommunicated in September 1993 though he remains committed to the LDS faith.

Given the changes in revelation, it may be hard to grasp the conviction with which Mormon apologist Hugh Nibley claims "the gospel as the Mormons know it sprang full-grown from the words of Joseph Smith. It has never been worked over or touched up in any way and is free of revisions and alterations."[18]

Some early Mormons who found out about the alterations to divine texts left the church because they saw these changes as clear proof of Smith's lack of integrity. William McLellin, one early Mormon leader, wrote of his experience:

> In 1835 in Kirtland another committee was appointed to fix up the revelations for print again. I was teaching their high school in the lower room, the printing office being overhead. And I was often in Joseph's office, and know positively that some of the revelations were so altered, mutilated and changed that a good scholar would scarcely know them. In one revelation I counted 20 alterations! Hence, who can depend upon them? I cannot. I will not.... All your trouble arises from your taking that mutilated and altered Doctrine and Covenants.[19]

The most important reality about Doctrine and Covenants for contemporary debate is that the texts themselves prove that Joseph Smith was the kind of person who would alter alleged divine revelation. The easiest way to settle this is to look for oneself at the differences between early and later versions of this or that particular revelation. On this, the Tanners have simplified the process by noting additions, deletions, and alterations in various sections of Doctrine and Covenants. The image below shows the alterations made in an original revelation in order for it to match the finished product in the later printing of the revelation. In this case, it involves Book of Commandments Chapter 4 with Section 5:1-11 of Doctrine and Covenants. The changes speak for themselves. This example can be duplicated many times with other sections of Doctrine and Covenants.

BOOK OF COMMANDMENTS - Chapter 4
COMPARE DOCTRINE AND COVENANTS - Sec. 5:1-11

W.A. = Words Added
W.D. = Words Deleted
T.C. = Textual Change

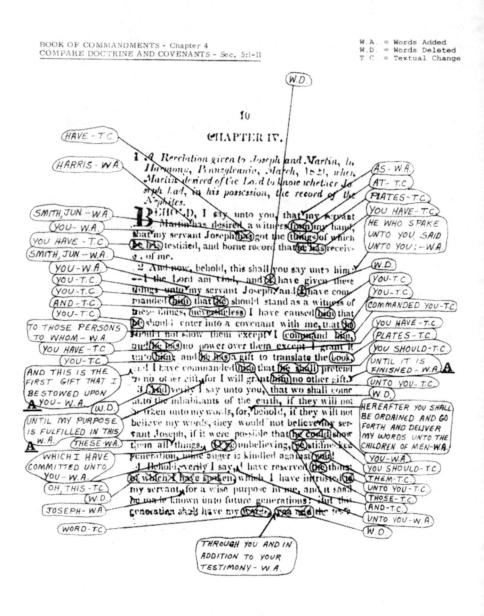

The Pearl of Great Price

In late June and early July 1835, the Mormon community of Kirtland, Ohio was abuzz with the visit of a traveling merchant named Michael Chandler. The salesman was touring America with an exhibit of four mummies and some papyri from ancient Egypt. No one would have predicted that the material would become the most famous and most controversial of Mormon writings.

These ancient artifacts have been traced to Giovanni Pietro Antonio Lebolo (b. 1781), onetime associate to Bernardino Drovetti (1776–1852), the French consul general to Egypt in the early part of the nineteenth century. After Lebolo died, his Egyptian collection was sent to New York and eventually wound up with Chandler.

The Egyptian material fascinated Joseph Smith, and he announced that the papyri contained the actual writings of the patriarch Abraham. He also said there was original material from Joseph, son of Isaac, another Old Testament figure. Smith translated the first part of the Abrahamic document in 1835 and finished the rest in early 1842. It was printed in the Mormon *Times and Seasons* in two installments in the spring of 1842 (March 1: Abraham 1:1–2:18 and March 15: Abraham 2:19–5:21). In addition to the translation, the LDS publication also contained three illustrations (facsimiles) from the Egyptian papyrus itself.

In addition to the Bible, Book of Mormon, and Doctrine and Covenants, the LDS church accepts the Pearl of Great Price (PGP) as sacred scripture. The shortest in the Mormon canon, the PGP was originally published in England in 1851 through the efforts of the British mission leader Franklin Richards. The American edition came out in

1878. The PGP was affirmed as a "standard work" or scripture at the LDS General Conferences in 1880 and 1890.

The contents of the volume changed a bit over the decades. A few minor items were removed and some material was transferred to the Doctrine and Covenants, most notably what is now section 132 on plural marriage. Both Joseph Smith's Celestial Kingdom vision from 1836 and Joseph F. Smith's 1918 vision on redemption of the dead were added to PGP in 1976 but then transferred to the Doctrine and Covenants work three years later.[1]

Currently the PGP contains five items:

1. Selections from the Book of Moses

2. The Book of Abraham

3. Joseph Smith—Matthew

4. Joseph Smith—History

5. The Articles of Faith

"Selections from the Book of Moses" is a direct borrowing from the Joseph Smith's Inspired Translation of the Bible, a revision of the King James Version of the Bible by Smith, which has significant changes. In this case, the selections are from the first part of the Book of Genesis. The Inspired Translation was begun on June 1830. Smith translated the first twenty-four chapters of Genesis, then switched to the New Testament, and then returned to translating the rest of the Old Testament. The Selections from the Book of Moses are from Genesis 1:1–8:18.

The Selections duplicates the wording of the King James Version on most verses but also makes additions to the text that are very significant for LDS theology. For example, it is revealed to Moses that there are multiple worlds. Chapter one states: "And behold, the glory of the Lord was upon Moses, so that Moses stood in the presence of God, and talked with him face to face. And the Lord God said unto Moses: For mine own purpose have I made these things....And by the word of my power, have I created them, which is mine Only Begotten Son, who is full of grace and truth. And worlds without number have I created; and I also created them for mine own purpose; and by the Son I created them, which is mine Only Begotten."

The Book of Moses also teaches that the fall of Satan resulted from his pride and his plan to deny humans free choice.

> And I, the Lord God, spake unto Moses, saying: That Satan, whom thou hast commanded in the name of mine Only Begotten, is the same which was from the beginning, and he came before me, saying—Behold, here am I, send me, I will be thy son, and I will redeem all mankind, that one soul shall not be lost, and surely I will do it; wherefore give me thine honor. But, behold, my Beloved Son, which was my Beloved and Chosen from the beginning, said unto me—Father, thy will be done, and the glory be thine forever. Wherefore, because that Satan rebelled against me, and sought to destroy the agency of man, which I, the Lord God, had given him, and also, that I should give unto him mine own power; by the power of mine Only Begotten, I caused that he should be cast down. (4:1-4)

Both the Articles of Faith and "Joseph Smith—History" are taken from the pages of the 7 volume *History of the Church*. The first six volumes cover the life of Smith while the last deals with the period from Smith's death until 1848.[2] The Articles of Faith were penned by Joseph Smith in 1842 and were originally an appendage to a letter sent to Chicago editor John Wentworth. The Articles were printed in the Mormon newspaper *Times and Seasons* in March 1842 and later put into the Pearl of Great Price. The "Joseph Smith—History" material is a brief account of Smith's life, the First Vision, and the discovery and publication of the Book of Mormon.

The "Joseph Smith—Matthew" part of the Pearl of Great Price is a selection from Smith's Inspired Translation of basically one chapter of the Gospel of Matthew.

The Book of Abraham

The Book of Abraham is the most significant and controversial part of the Pearl of Great Price and will be the focus of the remainder of this chapter and the next. The following timeline is a slight adaptation of the careful investigation of the Book of Abraham by Michael Marquardt.[3] Smith used various scribes in his translation work as the chronology below states. Marquardt also notes Smith's attempts at learning Hebrew and Greek, which bear some relation to his translation of the Egyptian material.

1835	
June 30	Michael H. Chandler arrives in Kirtland, Ohio
July 6	Chandler gives Smith a certificate relating to his knowledge of the writings.
July 7–31	Smith, Cowdery, and Phelps work on "Egyptian Alphabet."
October 1	Smith, Cowdery, and Phelps work on the astronomy portion of the "Egyptian Alphabet"
October 3, 19, 24, 29	Smith exhibits the Egyptian artifacts and offers explanations of their meaning.
October 7	Smith, and presumably Phelps, recommences translating the ancient Egyptian records.
October 29	Parrish starts writing for Smith.
November 14	Revelation for Parrish to be a scribe.
November 17, 23, 30	Smith exhibits the Egyptian artifacts and offers explanations of their meaning.
November 19, 20, 24, 25, 26	Smith spends most of each day "translating," and on the 26th "transcribing" the Egyptian records.
November 20, 21, 23, 27	Cowdery returns from New York with books. Smith studies Hebrew.
December 4–5, 7–8, 14, 26, 30	Smith studies Hebrew.
December 7, 10, 12, 14–16, 20, 23	Smith exhibits the Egyptian artifacts and offers explanations of their meaning.
December 23	Smith studies Greek.
1836	
January 12, 30	Smith exhibits the Egyptian artifacts.
January 4–6, 8–9, 14, 18–21	Smith attends Hebrew school.

January 26	Joshua Seixas of Hudson, Ohio, arrives in Kirtland to teach Hebrew.
February 3, 11, 16	Smith exhibits the Egyptian records.
March 29	Last day of Hebrew school taught by Seixas.
March 27	Dedication of the Kirtland temple.
1842	
February 19	The first installment of "Book of Abraham" is typeset for publication in the *Times and Seasons* (Nauvoo, Illinois).
February 23	Smith gives engraver Reuben Hedlock instructions to make a cut (or engraving) "for the altar & Gods in the Records of Abraham" for the *Times and Seasons*.
February 24	Smith explains the records of Abraham.
March 1	This issue of the *Times and Seasons* prints Abraham 1:1–2:18, plus Facsimile No. 1.
March 2	Smith proofs the *Times and Seasons* (issue dated March 1); issue is mailed ca. March 4.
March 4	Smith exhibits the original papyrus to Hedlock for several illustrations, and gives instructions for engraving Facsimile No. 2.
March 8	Smith commences translating for next issue of the *Times and Seasons*.
March 9	Smith continues translating "Book of Abraham."
March 15	This issue of the *Times and Seasons* prints Abraham 2:19–5:21, plus Facsimile No. 2. The issue is mailed ca. March 19.
May 16	This issue of the *Times and Seasons* prints Facsimile No. 3.

Contents

The Book of Abraham translation in the Pearl of Great Price contains five chapters. It is prefaced by this notice: "Translated from the Papyrus, by Joseph Smith A Translation of some ancient Records that have fallen into our hands from the catacombs of Egypt. The writings of Abraham while he was in Egypt, called the Book of Abraham, written by his own hand, upon papyrus."[4] (See *History of the Church*, 2:235–36, 348–51.)

The account begins with Abraham's announcement: "In the land of the Chaldeans, at the residence of my fathers, I, Abraham, saw that it was needful for me to obtain another place of residence;" His reason for departing was due to the idolatry of the people (1:1–15). He was almost sacrificed by pagan priests on an altar but God intervened (1:8–19). Abraham provides an illustration of the altar for his readers. It is shown as Facsimile 1 in the Book of Abraham. Abraham provides the names of some of the gods in the chapter and in the explanation to the drawings in the Facsimile. They are Elkenah, Libnah, Mahmackrah, Korash, and Pharaoh.

Chapter 2 tells the journey of Abraham and Sarai to Haran and then on to Canaan. A famine forces a further move to Egypt. God told Abraham to introduce his wife as his sister in order to spare his life from Egyptians. The chapter also gives details about the Abrahamic Covenant (2:6–11). Verse 11 is significant because of its emphasis on the priesthood, a theme that was central in Smith's developing ecclesiology.

Chapter 3 reports a vision received by Abraham concerning the sun, moon, and stars. God tells Abraham that he lives near a star named Kolob (3:9). He is also told about the eternal nature of spirits, life before humanity's arrival on earth, and God's choice of the Son of Man as redeemer (3:27) instead of another, presumably Lucifer. Abraham provides a second illustration or Facsimile to provide further data on the stars, planets, and God's rule.

Chapters 4 and 5 present a creation narrative that parallels the Genesis account except that the Book of Abraham advances a plurality of Gods. Thus, 4:1–3 reads:

1 And then the Lord said: Let us go down. And they went down at the beginning, and they, that is the Gods, organized and formed the heavens and the earth.

2 And the earth, after it was formed, was empty and desolate, because they had not formed anything but the earth; and darkness reigned upon the face of the deep, and the Spirit of the Gods was brooding upon the face of the waters.

3 And they (the Gods) said: Let there be light; and there was light."

After Adam is created the text in chapter 5 states:

14 And the Gods said: Let us make an help meet for the man, for it is not good that the man should be alone, therefore we will form an help meet for him.

15 And the Gods caused a deep sleep to fall upon Adam; and he slept, and they took one of his ribs, and closed up the flesh in the stead thereof;

16 And of the rib which the Gods had taken from man, formed they a woman, and brought her unto the man.

Importance

In contrast to the Bible, Book of Mormon, and Doctrine and Covenants, the Book of Abraham is a short scripture. However, it remains very significant for several reasons.

First, key verses in chapter 1 contributed to racism theories that were advanced later in Mormon history. After describing his rescue by God, Abraham makes some observations about the king of Egypt and the origins of king and country.

Now this king of Egypt was a descendant from the loins of Ham, and was a partaker of the blood of the Canaanites by birth.... From this descent sprang all the Egyptians, and thus the blood of the Canaanites was preserved in the land. The land of Egypt being first discovered by a woman, who was the daughter of Ham, and the daughter of Egyptus, which in the Chaldean signifies Egypt, which signifies that which is forbidden; When this woman discovered the land it was under water, who afterward settled her sons in it; and thus, from Ham, sprang that race which preserved the curse in the land. (1:21–24)

In later Mormon writing this text was used to justify denying the priesthood to blacks and to justify a common racist view of the day that black skin is a curse tied to Ham and his descendants.[5] The ban on blacks holding the priesthood was lifted in June 1978 by Spencer W. Kimball, the LDS prophet at the time. As with some Protestant denominations in the nineteenth century, Mormon leaders used their sacred texts to provide divine justification for racist views and actions.[6]

Second, the Book of Abraham has enormous importance because of its teaching about the dwelling place of God, various items in cosmology, the pre-earthly existence of humans, and the choice of Jesus as redeemer. This is the only place in all of LDS scripture where Kolob, near the dwelling place of God, is mentioned. The text of the Book of Abraham does not state whether there are people living on Kolob. In spite of the absence of a lot of details, Mormons continue to sing a hymn about Kolob in their Sunday worship.[7] Chapter 3 of the Book of Abraham provides the most extensive discussion in the LDS canon of the stars, sun, moon, and planets, though the teaching is very unclear, as LDS scholars admit.[8] The teachings on humanity's pre-earthly existence parallel various passages in both Doctrine and Covenants and the Book of Moses.[9] In the end LDS members have three human authorities for their unique views of creation and humanity's place in it: Joseph Smith, Moses, and Abraham.

Third, the Book of Abraham is significant in light of its teaching on the plurality of Gods. The Book of Abraham adopts a polytheistic explanation for creation, as seen in chapters 4 and 5. This alternative to monotheism created a shock for both traditional Christians and some Mormons in the days of Joseph Smith.[10] LDS scholars deny that the Church teaches polytheism; however passages clearly do reference gods.[11]

Fourth, the mention of the "grand Key-words of the Priesthood" (from explanatory note 7 of Facsimile 2), became significant immediately because these words coincided with Joseph's growing emphasis on the priesthood through the 1830s. There was little focus on priesthood when the Mormon Church was founded in 1830. However, starting in 1831 Smith and other LDS leaders gave the priesthood much greater attention. Thus, the mention of priesthood in the Book of Abraham fit with a developing concept in LDS thought and practice.

Overall, the early Mormons marveled at Joseph's remarkable ability to take ancient Egyptian and put it into plain English. Both prophet and people credited God for the translation of the Book of Abraham. However, problems arose when Egyptologists were finally able to see the papyri.

The Book of Abraham

Mormons at the time greeted Joseph Smith's translation of the Egyptian texts with excitement. They were confident that Joseph had a supernatural gift because he translated the gold plates of the Book of Mormon. They believed that this same gift aided him in translating the Egyptian papyrus. The arrival and translation of the documents were considered to be evidence of the providence of God.

Smith had several men around him who served as his scribes or secretaries. They took dictation on both mundane and spiritual matters, including transcribing Smith's revelations. W.W. Phelps was one of Smith's scribes. Phelps wrote to his wife about the Egyptian documents: in mid-July 1835:

> As no one could translate these writings, they were presented to President Smith. He soon knew what they were and said they … contained the sacred record kept of Joseph in Pharaoh's court in Egypt, and the teachings of Father Abraham. God has so ordered it that these mummies and writings have been brought in the Church … These records of old times, when we translate and print them in a book, will make a good witness for the Book of Mormon.[1]

One can only imagine the impression that both the papyri and translation must have made on the first Mormon witnesses. Some might have been bewildered by the strange Egyptian language and drawings. Later they might have been amazed by the clarity of Joseph's translation. Consider the first drawing or facsimile that Smith coped from the Egyptian papyrus, for example.[2]

Mormons would have imagined that the image represented the sacrifice of Abraham mentioned in chapter 1 of the book of Abraham. Joseph gave a detailed explanation. Twelve numbers were placed on the image:

1. The Angel of the Lord

2. Abraham fastened upon an altar

3. The idolatrous priest of Elkenah attempting to offer up Abraham as a sacrifice

4. The altar for sacrifice by the idolatrous priests, standing before the gods of Elkenah, Libnah, Mahmackrah, Korash, and Pharaoh

5. The idolatrous god of Elkenah

6. The idolatrous god of Libnah

7. The idolatrous god of Mahmackrah

8. The idolatrous god of Korash

9. The idolatrous god of Pharaoh

10. Abraham in Egypt

11. Designed to represent the pillars of heaven, as understood by the Egyptians

12. Raukeeyang, signifying expanse, or the firmament over our heads; but in this case, in relation to this subject, the Egyptians meant it to signify Shaumau, to be high, or the heavens, answering to the Hebrew word, Shaumahyeem

Facsimile 2 would have been more puzzling to the first onlookers since there is nothing in the image that links easily or directly to the written text.

Twenty-one items were numbered this time with explanation. Here is an abbreviated version:

1. Kolob, signifying the first creation, nearest to the celestial, or the residence of God

2. Stands next to Kolob, called by the Egyptians Oliblish

3. Representing also the grand Key-words of the Holy Priesthood, as revealed to Adam in the Garden of Eden, as also to Seth, Noah, Melchizedek, Abraham, and all to whom the Priesthood was revealed

4. Answers to the Hebrew word Raukeeyang, signifying expanse, or the firmament of the heavens

5. Is called in Egyptian Enish-go-on-dosh

6. Represents this earth in its four quarters

7. Represents God sitting upon his throne, revealing through

the heavens the grand Key-words of the Priesthood; as, also, the sign of the Holy Ghost unto Abraham, in the form of a dove

8. Contains writings that cannot be revealed unto the world; but is to be had in the Holy Temple of God

9. Ought not to be revealed at the present time

10. Also. If the world can find out these numbers, so let it be. Amen.

11. Figures 12, 13, 14, 15, 16, 17, 18, 19, 20, and 21, will be given in the own due time of the Lord

Facsimile 3 is somewhat similar to the first drawing but would still be somewhat of a mystery to the first Mormons:

1. Abraham sitting upon Pharaoh's throne, by the politeness of the king, with a crown upon his head, representing the Priesthood, as emblematical of the grand Presidency in Heaven; with the scepter of justice and judgment in his hand

2. King Pharaoh, whose name is given in the characters above his head

3. Signifies Abraham in Egypt as given also in Figure 10 of Facsimile No. 1.

4. Prince of Pharaoh, King of Egypt, as written above the hand

5. Shulem, one of the king's principal waiters, as represented by the characters above his hand

6. Olimlah, a slave belonging to the prince

As one might expect, non-Mormons questioned Joseph's claims about the papyri. William S. West, a native of Braceville, Ohio, traveled to Kirtland to see the display. He wrote later:

They say that the mummies were Egyptian, but the records are those of Abraham and Joseph ... Is it possible that a record written by Abraham, and another by Joseph, containing the most important revelation that God ever gave to man, should be entirely lost by the tenacious Israelites, and preserved by the unbelieving Egyptians, and by them embalmed and deposited in the catacombs with an Egyptian priest[?] ... I venture to say no, it is not possible. It is more likely that the records are those of the Egyptians.[3]

The scepticism of West and others like him did not shake the belief of faithful Mormons. However, genuine troubles emerged three decades later. In 1856 copies of the facsimiles were shown to Theodule Deveria, an Egyptologist at the Louvre in Paris. He announced that the illustrations had nothing to do with Abraham but involved Egyptian funeral rites.[4] Mormon Church leaders in Utah greeted the academic's view with disdain. Instead of re-examining their conclusions, they significantly changed the introduction to the Book of Abraham: the words "purporting to be" (the writings of Abraham) were dropped from the preface and it has read ever since: "The writings of Abraham while he was in Egypt, called the Book of Abraham, written by his own hand upon papyrus." Then, the LDS leaders ratified the Book of Abraham as part of the sacred canon of the Mormon Church. This represents one of the greatest intellectual blunders in LDS history.

Criticism died down until 1912 when Franklin S. Spaulding, the Episcopal Bishop of Utah, released a pamphlet under the title "Joseph Smith Jr., As a Translator." The heart of this document involved replies from Egyptologists about the three facsimiles. Their comments about Smith's translation were derisive:

> It may be safely said that there is not one single word that is true in these explanations.... None but the ignorant could possibly be imposed on by such ludicrous blunders." Dr. W. M. Flinders Petrie, London University.[5]
>
> The 'Book of Abraham,' it is hardly necessary to say, is a pure fabrication. Cuts 1 and 3 are inaccurate copies of well-known scenes on funeral papyri, and cut 2 is a copy of one of the magical discs which in the late Egyptian period were placed under the heads of mummies ... Joseph Smith's interpretation of these cuts is a farrago of nonsense from beginning to end." Dr. Arthur C. Mace, Assistant Curator, Metropolitan Museum of Art, New York, Department of Egyptian Art.[6]
>
> "What he calls the 'Book of Abraham' is a funeral Egyptian text, probably not older than the Greek ages." Dr. Friedrich Freiheer von Bissing, [sic] Professor of Egyptology in the University of Munich.[7]
>
> "It is difficult to deal seriously with Joseph Smith's impudent fraud. His facsimile from the Book of Abraham No. 2 is an ordinary hypocephalus ... Number 3 is a representation of the Goddess Maat leading the Pharaoh before Osiris, behind whom stands the Goddess Isis. Smith has turned the Goddess into a king and Osiris into Abraham." Dr. A. H. Sayce, Oxford, England.[8]

The Mormon response was handled by several figures, including Robert C. Webb, PhD. It turns out he had no doctorate and his real name was J. E. Homans. Under his pseudonym, he wrote scholarly sounding articles against Spaulding. Egyptologists dismissed his work, but Webb and some key Mormon intellectuals (B. H. Roberts, for example) managed to calm troubled Mormon minds.[9] There were no original documents to examine at the time. It was thought that the papyri had been destroyed in a Chicago fire in 1871.

In 1966 some of the Egyptian material was discovered at the Metropolitan Museum of Art, and the LDS church got ownership the next year.

After the discovery of these portions of the Book of Abraham, study by non-Mormon Egyptologists took off in earnest. Their conclusions have been unanimous: the papyri have nothing to do with Abraham or the Old Testament . The proper translation of the scrolls shows that they discuss funeral rites. Likewise, the three facsimiles are about specific and popular elements of Egyptian life and religion. There is nothing about Abraham, Old Testament priesthood, or any of the other detail given in Joseph's translation.

In 1968 Egyptologists John Wilson (University of Chicago), Richard Parker (Brown University), and Klaus Baer (Chicago) each adopted readings contradictory to Smith. A few LDS academics picked up the challenge to do their own work in Egyptology. One was Ed Ashment who went to the University of Chicago to learn Egyptian to defend his faith in the Book of Abraham. In an interview with PBS, his wife Nancy described the life-changing day when her husband sat down to translate Facsimile 2 and discovered what the text actually says:

> So he was busy working in the study, and I was in the kitchen fixing dinner; the boys were napping. And I heard funny sounds coming out of the study, and pretty soon I hear him in there just ranting and raving. I can tell he's very upset and I can't imagine what on earth he's upset about. So I went in and he had the Book of Abraham open on the desk in front of him and he had papers and he's translating, he's got dictionaries out. And he looks at it and he says: "This is not what they say it is at all. This has nothing to do with Abraham. This is about a little girl who died. I mean, it's a papyrus that was put under her head, and it has nothing to do with Abraham." And we were both devastated.[10]

Other LDS academics who learned Egyptian have preserved their faith by adopting new explanations to reconcile their trust in the integrity of Joseph's translation with intellectual analysis of the papyrus. Michael Rhodes, John Gee and Kerry Muhlestein are the leading figures in this regard.[11]

Robert Ritner, a professor at the University of Chicago, is the most notable scholar involved in recent translation of the Egyptian material. A student of Baer, Ritner published *The Joseph Smith Papyri* in 2012. The work includes the most detailed textual analysis and translation ever done on the papyrus. Ritner is blunt about Smith's lack of knowledge of ancient Egypt. He notes: "Facsimile 3 provides indisputable evidence that Smith *had absolutely no abilities* to read or translate Egyptian, or even derive accurate information from Egyptian images. He could not distinguish deities from humans, females from males or even human from animal figures."[12] He also responds to the claim by Mormon scholars that parts of the papyri have been lost. He concludes:

> The fact that Smith's published interpretation of the papyrus is pure fantasy is indication not of a lost papyrus or section, but of the *ultimate source* of Smith's wording—his imagination. Since *there is agreement* that Smith could not translate accurately the hieroglyphs on Facsimile 3—despite his published claims to the contrary—there is no reason to believe that he could have translated any supposedly lost section of the papyrus with greater accuracy.[13]

Not surprisingly, Ritner is very tough on prominent Mormon academics who defend the Book of Abraham at all costs. He critiques Hugh Nibley, the most famous LDS apologist, for failure to follow the evidence and resorting to personal attacks on Egyptologists. At one point Ritner condemns "Nibley"s nihilistic quibbling on the impossibility of true translation" and adds that "Nibley can only defend Smith's use of the term "translation" by undercutting the very meaning of the term."[14]

Of others he writes: "Except for those willfully blind, the case is closed. As an episode in American religious history and early "Egyptomania, the text is still of interest; no investigator seeking ancient evidence should waste his time."[15]

Most Mormons do not know about the problems with the Book of Abraham. Others realize there is controversy and take comfort that there are LDS scholars who know Egyptian and still trust Joseph's translation. Four things remain problematic for supporters of the Book of Abraham:

1. In order for LDS scholars familiar with the Egyptian language to account for the differences between the Book of Abraham and the Egyptian documents themselves, they have been forced to resort to the desperate argument that the scrolls discovered at the Metropolitan are

not the ones Joseph used. However, enormous problems can be seen by simple analysis of the three facsimiles referenced by Smith in the text of the Book of Abraham itself. Even a minimal investigation of these shows that Smith was given no revelation from God about their content and meaning. Early Mormons had no opportunity to look at similar facsimiles to those Joseph used in the Book of Abraham. They were fooled by their blind trust in his prophetic status, not to mention his audacity in providing incredible though completely false detail about the facsimiles.

2. The Book of Abraham shows anachronistic elements indicating that it was Smith's creation. For example, the comments on astrology are what one would expect from a nineteenth century American hand, as Grant Palmer shows in his book *An Insider's View of Mormon Origins*.[16] Palmer mentions that Thomas Dick's *Philosophy of a Future State* (2nd ed. 1830) has ideas parallel to the Book of Abraham including the notion of eternal intelligences and the throne of God as a centre of the universe.[17]

3. To be blunt, Smith's interpretation of the material bears absolutely no relation to the elements of Egyptian religion that appear in the papyri. Granted, much of the debate about the Book of Abraham involves enormous technical details. Mormon apologists hope that the complexities involved lead LDS members to simply trust the Church in its acceptance of the Book of Abraham. After all, how many people know Egyptian?

Regardless of language skills, some things are patently obvious as proof that Smith was either deluded or lying about the Book of Abraham. Consider illustration seven in facsimile 2.

Joseph Smith claimed that the picture there represents God giving revelation about the restoration of the priesthood. Smith is totally wrong. The image given on the papyrus is the Egyptian god Min who, with erect penis, is being approached by a snake, also with an erect penis. Smith obviously knew nothing about pagan Egyptian religion. Mormon scholars know this detail and engage in torturous arguments to defend Smith at all costs. The Church even altered the facsimile in one edition of the Book of Abraham so that no penis was shown.[18]

4. Egyptologists over the last century and a half (represented by Deveria, Spaulding's contacts, Baer and company, and now Ritner) have

all agreed that Joseph's handling of the facsimiles is evidence of his utter failure to understand Egyptian language and culture.[19] They have also agreed that the papyrus is from a time period long after Abraham lived. So, there is a failure by Joseph Smith in relation to both the nature and dating of the material purchased by the Church in 1835.

The LDS prophets and Church authorities have remained silent regarding evidence that the Book of Abraham is a fraud. The book remains part of LDS scripture and is still described on an official LDS website as "a translation from some Egyptian papyri that came into the hands of Joseph Smith in 1835, containing writings of the patriarch Abraham."[20]

In spite of the silence from leadership, there are signs that the church might be moving away from its dogmatism. In 2009 John Gee claimed that "the Book of Abraham is not central to the restored gospel of Christ."[21] Gee claimed that the Book was quoted less than 1 percent of the time in General Conference messages and concluded: "How the Book of Abraham was translated is unimportant. The Church does not stand or fall on the Book of Abraham."[22]

Unfortunately, Gee's comments are misleading. The Book of Abraham is crucial in thinking about the restored gospel since the document offers clear proof that Joseph Smith engaged in fraud or deception. How Joseph bungled his translation is important, regardless of what Gee claims. Otherwise, why have Mormon apologists worked so hard at defending his translation? Finally, the fall of the Book of Abraham goes a long way to proving that the foundations of Mormonism are crumbling.

God and Many Gods

"We believe in God, the Eternal Father, and in His Son, Jesus Christ, and in the Holy Ghost." —*Articles of Faith*

There are major theological issues where traditional Christians and Mormons are in total agreement. Both groups affirm the historicity of the miracles of Jesus, the sacrificial nature of his death, and the reality of his bodily resurrection. Conservative Christians and Mormons also uphold similar standards of morality: sanctity of life, value of marriage, opposition to homosexual activity, obedience to government, opposition to gambling and pornography Despite these basic similarities there are significant differences, as has been noted previously. The most serious questions arise about matters of continuity between the Bible and other LDS standard works and over how God is understood in the two faith traditions.

This chapter discusses two questions: (1) Do the Latter-day Saints believe in more than one God? and (2) Does the Mormon Church teach that God the Father used to be a man?

One God in Mormon Doctrine

Do Mormons believe in more than one God? To many Latter-day Saints this is a strange question. After all, the Articles of Faith state: "We believe in God."[1]

In addition to the statement in the Articles of Faith, Mormons pray in the same way as traditional Christians—to one God: "Our Father, who art in Heaven."[2] Official LDS websites consistently affirm belief in one God and the Book of Mormon is absolutely clear on the matter:

And Zeezrom said unto him: Thou sayest there is a true and living God? And Amulek said: Yea, there is a true and living God. Now, Zeezrom said: Is there more than one God? And he answered, No. Now Zeezrom said unto him again: How knowest thou these things? And he said: An angel hath made them known unto me. (Alma 11:26-31)

The following chart outlines texts from both the Book of Mormon and Doctrine and Covenants that affirm the idea of monotheism.

One God in the Book of Mormon and Doctrine and Covenants

Book of Mormon

Testimony of the Three Witnesses	"And the honor be to the Father, and to the Son, and to the Holy Ghost, which is one God."
1 Nephi 13:41	"for there is one God and one Shepherd over all the earth."
2 Nephi 31:21	"behold, this is the doctrine of Christ, and the only and true doctrine of the Father, and of the Son, and of the Holy Ghost, which is one God, without end. Amen."
Mosiah 15:4	"And they are one God, yea, the very Eternal Father of heaven and of earth."
Alma 11:28-29	"Now Zeezrom said: Is there more than one God? And he answered, No."
Alma 11:44b	"everything shall be ... arraigned before the bar of Christ the Son, and God the Father, and the Holy Spirit, which is one Eternal God."
Alma 14:5a	"And the people ... testified that there was but one God, and that he should send his Son among the people."
3 Nephi 11:27	"And after this manner shall ye baptize in my name; for behold, verily I say unto you, that the Father, and the Son, and the Holy Ghost are one; and I am in the Father, and the Father in me, and the Father and I are one."
Mormon 7:7	[the redeemed will] "sing ceaseless praises with the choirs above, unto the Father, and unto the Son, and unto the Holy Ghost, which are one God, in a state of happiness which hath no end."
Ether 2:8	"whoso should possess this land of promise, from that time henceforth and forever, should serve him, the true and only God.

Doctrine & Covenants

20:19	"And gave unto them commandments that they should love and serve him, the only living and true God, and that he should be the only being whom they should worship."
20:28	"Which Father, Son, and Holy Ghost are one God, infinite and eternal, without end. Amen."

The Articles of Faith and the Book of Mormon agree with biblical testimony found in the prophets, the Gospels, and the letters of Paul:

- "Ye *are* my witnesses, saith the Lord, and my servant whom I have chosen: that ye may know and believe me, and understand that I *am* he: before me there was no God formed, neither shall there be after me." (Isa. 43:10 KJV)

- And this is life eternal, that they might know thee the only true God, and Jesus Christ, whom thou hast sent." (John 17:3 KJV)

- "One God and Father of all, who *is* above all, and through all, and in you all."(Eph. 4:6 KJV)

However, there are other factors that indicate the LDS affirmation of monotheism is not so straightforward. First, current LDS leadership teaches that the Father, Son, and Holy Ghost are three separate Gods. Apostle Jeffrey Holland of the Quorum of the Twelve Apostles stated at an LDS October 2007 General Conference:

We declare it is self-evident from the scriptures that the Father, the Son, and the Holy Ghost are separate persons, three divine beings ... who [constitute] a single Godhead ... united in purpose, in manner, in testimony, in mission ... [but not] ... three persons combined in one substance, a Trinitarian notion never set forth in the scriptures because it is not true."[3]

Holland went on to say that the Trinitarian "formulation for divinity is truly incomprehensible."[4] Meanwhile, even if we accept Holland's explanation of one Godhood as a form of monotheism a larger complication remains.[5] Various texts in LDS scripture affirm the existence of gods/Gods beyond Father, Son, and Spirit. As well, Joseph Smith explicitly taught a plurality of gods before his death. We have already noted references in the Book of Abraham that speak of the role of the "gods" in creation.[6]

In addition to the Book of Abraham, the Doctrine and Covenants has polytheistic overtones in Section 121. The text states that there is a time coming when "nothing shall be withheld, whether there be one God or many gods" (v. 28). Verse 32 speaks of "the Council of the Eternal God of all other gods."

Beyond LDS Scriptural texts, Joseph Smith can be credited with the most explicit early Mormon advocacy of a plurality of gods. In his famous 1844 sermon at a memorial for King Follett, a Mormon leader, Smith stated that "in the beginning, the head of the Gods called a council of the Gods."[7]

This is a clear parallel to Doctrine and Covenants 121. In a later sermon, just eleven days before his death, Smith stated: "I will preach on the plurality of Gods. I have selected this text for that express purpose. I wish to declare I have always and in all congregations when I have preached on the subject of the Deity, it has been the plurality of Gods."[8] He states that the Father, Son and Spirit are "three Gods" and then goes on to state that a Trinitarian understanding of God would be "a curious organization" and "a wonderfully big God—he would be a giant or a monster."[9]

Smith's explicit polytheism opened the way for later Mormon leaders to argue for the existence of many gods. Orson Pratt (1811-1881), a prominent Apostle, stated in a sermon in February 1855: "If we should take a million of worlds like this and number their particles, we should find that there are more Gods than there are particles of matter in those worlds."[10] Brigham Young, the second LDS prophet, stated in the Salt Lake Tabernacle: "How many Gods there are, I do not know. But there never was a time when there were not Gods."[11]

So, while the Bible and the Book of Mormon clearly teach monotheism, it is obvious that Smith moved away from this stance as he penned certain verses in both Doctrine and Covenants and the Book of Abraham. These polytheistic sentiments reached full flower in two of his sermons just before his death. This promotion of polytheism has been dominant in LDS history until the late twentieth century.

God and Many Gods

The Nature of God in Mormon Theology

LDS affirmation of one God is also complicated by clear evidence that Mormonism teaches that God was once a man. Mormons give frequent affirmation that God is eternal, but the issue is complicated within their writings. The Book of Mormon posits a traditional view that God has always been God. The clearest passage reads: "For I know that God is not a partial God, neither a changeable being; but he is unchangeable from all eternity to all eternity." (Moroni 8:18)[12] This understanding of God fits with biblical teaching. For example, "For I *am* the Lord, I do not change; therefore you are not consumed, O Sons of Jacob (Malachi 3:6 NKJV),

Additionally, material in the Doctrine and Covenants fits with traditional Christian theology. "By these things we know that there is a God in heaven, who is infinite and eternal, from everlasting to everlasting the same unchangeable God, the framer of heaven and earth, and all things which are in them"(20:17). A later chapter reads: "Father, Son, and Holy Ghost are one God, infinite and eternal, without end. Amen." (20:28)

Yet over time Joseph Smith's view of God shifted.[13] By the time of his death, Smith argued that God the Father used to be a man. His most famous declaration is found in the King Follett discourse:

> God himself was once as we are now, and is an exalted man, and sits enthroned in yonder heavens! That is the great secret ... I am going to tell you how God came to be God. We have imagined and supposed that God was God from all eternity. I will refute that idea, and take away the veil, so that you may see.[14]

That God the Father progressed to Godhood is probably the most radical teaching ever introduced by Smith. Smith's advocacy of a temporal, finite God shifted the Mormon paradigm away from that of traditional Christianity.[15] Brigham Young adopted this view as have other LDS prophets and leaders since the earliest days of Mormonism. The following chart provides quotes from LDS leaders on God the Father's progression from man to God.

LDS leaders	Quotes on God the Father once a man	Source and date
Joseph Smith Jr.	"God himself was once as we are now, and is an exalted Man, and sits enthroned in yonder heavens. That is the great secret."	1844, "King Follett Discourse," Speech originally given April 7, 1844
Orson Pratt	"We were begotten by our Father in Heaven; the person of our Father in Heaven was begotten on a previous heavenly world by His Father; and again, He was begotten by a still more ancient Father; and so on."	1853–1854, The Seer, p. 132
Orson Pratt	"The Gods who dwell in the Heaven ... were once in a fallen state ... they were exalted also, from fallen men to Celestial Gods."	1853–1854, The Seer, p. 23
Orson Hyde	"Remember that God, our heavenly Father, was perhaps once a child ... and rose step by step in the scale of progress."	1854, Journal of Discourses, 1:23
Wilford Woodruff	"God himself is increasing and progressing in knowledge, power, and dominion, and will do so, worlds without end"	1859, Journal of Discourses, 6:120
Brigham Young	"He [God] is our Father—the Father of our spirits, and was once a man in mortal flesh as we are, and is now an exalted being. How many Gods there are, I do not know. But there never was a time when there were not Gods"	1860, Journal of Discourses, 7:333
Milton R. Hunter	"Mormon prophets have continuously taught the sublime truth that God the Eternal Father was once a mortal man who passed through a school of earth life similar to that through which we are now passing. He became God—an exalted being—through obedience to the same eternal Gospel truths that we are given opportunity today to obey"	1958, *The Gospel Through the Ages,* p. 104

Milton R. Hunter	"[W]e must accept the fact that there was a time when Deity was much less powerful than He is today... he grew in experience and continued to grow until He attained the status of Godhood"	1958, *The Gospel Through the Ages*, p. 114–15
Bruce R. McConkie	" ... as the Prophet also taught, there is 'a God above the Father of our Lord Jesus Christ'"	1966, *Mormon Doctrine*, p. 322
John A. Widtsoe	"...God must have been engaged from the beginning... in progressive development, and infinite as God is, he must have been less powerful in the past than he is today."	1968, *A Rational Theology as Taught by the Church of Jesus Christ of Latter-day Saints*, p. 24

The Mormon understanding of deity departs from traditional Christianity in two other respects. First, LDS leaders teach that God the Father has a physical body. Joseph's First Vision is explicit; both Father and Son were in bodily form. For Mormons, Joseph's first vision trumps the dictum of Jesus that "God is a Spirit" (John 4:24). Smith's teaching of an embodied God is illustrated in the Book of Abraham where God is said to dwell near the planet Kolob. (3:3)[16]

Second, LDS leaders also teach that there is a Heavenly Mother, a wife to the Heavenly Father. Belief in a Heavenly Mother is affirmed by early Mormons and by contemporary LDS authorities. Some LDS leaders in the nineteenth century even taught that God the Father has many wives. Today Mormons are encouraged to be discrete in their conversation about the Mother in Heaven and are not to pray to her.[17] However, she has been referenced by LDS General Authorities over six hundred times since 1844.[18] The following chart provides material about her from various LDS leaders.

LDS leaders	Quote on heavenly Mother	Source and date
Eliza R. Snow	"When I leave this frail existence, When I lay this mortal by, Father, Mother, may I meet you, In your royal courts on high?"	*Times and Seasons* 17 (November 15, 1845), 1039.
W. W. Phelps	"Thy father is God, thy mother is the Queen of heaven, and so thy whole history, from eternity to eternity, is the laws, ordinances and truth of the 'Gods.'"	1844, Personal letter to William Smith on December 25, 1844.
George Q. Cannon	"The Latter-day Saints believe that God is an exalted Man, and that we are the offspring of Him and His wife."	1884, "Mr. Canon's [sic] Lecture," *Salt Lake Daily Herald*, April 15, 1884, p. 8.
Joseph F. Smith, John R. Winder, Anthon H. Lund	"All men and women are in the similitude of the universal Father and Mother and are literally the sons and daughters of Deity."	1909, *Improvement Era*, Nov. 1909, p. 75–81
LDS Church Manual	"By definition, exaltation includes the ability to procreate the family unit throughout eternity. This our Father in heaven has the power to do. His marriage partner is our mother in heaven."	1976, *Achieving a Celestial Marriage: Student Manual*, Church Educational Systems, p. 129.
Lorenzo Snow	"We have a mother in heaven. We are the offspring of God. He is our Father, and we have a Mother in the other life as well."	1984, *The Teachings of Lorenzo Snow*, ed. Clyde J. Williams, 1984, p. 191.
Lorenzo Snow	"Women can become like our mother in heaven.... we not only have a Father in 'that high and glorious place,' but that we have a Mother too; and you will become as great as your Mother, if you are faithful."	1984, *The Teachings of Lorenzo Snow*, ed. Clyde J. Williams, 1984, p. 7–8.
Gordon Hinckley	"Logic and reason would certainly suggest that if we have a Father in Heaven, we have a Mother in Heaven.... I regard it as inappropriate for anyone in the Church to pray to our Mother in Heaven."	1991, "Daughters of God," *Ensign* (Conference Edition), November 1991, p. 100.

Reed H. Bradford	"Everyone, before coming to this earth, lived with Heavenly Father and Heavenly Mother, and each was loved and taught by them as a member of their eternal family."	1992, *Encyclopedia of Mormonism*: Entry for "Family," p. 487
Elaine Anderson Cannon	"Latter-day Saints infer from authoritative sources of scripture and modern prophecy that there is a Heavenly Mother as well as a Heavenly Father."	1992, *Encyclopedia of Mormonism*: Entry for "Mother in Heaven", p. 487
Bruce McConkie	"Implicit in the Christian verity that all men are the spirit children of an Eternal Father is the usually unspoken truth that they are also the offspring of an Eternal Mother."	1996, Mormon Doctrine, p. 517

Regardless of whether or not God has a body or a wife, the LDS Church is faced with a dilemma concerning the fundamental nature of God. Either God is eternal (as the Bible, Book of Mormon, and most of the sections of Doctrine and Covenants teach) or he is not eternal (as Joseph Smith taught in his sermons and as later LDS authorities teach). The notion that God progressed from manhood to godhood has created internal disagreements among Mormons over whether God ever failed in his spiritual journey prior to exaltation.[19] Likewise, there is difficulty in the Mormon claim to be monotheists if God the Father has a God over him. All in all, Mormon scripture is contradictory in its description of the nature of God and even its dominant teaching of one eternal God is contradicted by Joseph Smith himself.

Jesus, Holy Spirit, and Humanity

For traditional Christians, official and popular LDS teaching that there are many Gods, that God the Father used to be a man, that God has a body, and that there is a Heavenly Mother raises extreme doubt about the basic integrity of Mormonism. For Christians, affirmation of monotheism and belief in an infinite eternal God are an essential part of biblical faith.

Further divergence arises when one considers teaching about Jesus, the Holy Spirit and humanity's relationship to the Godhead.: Again, Mormonism does not align with orthodox Christian faith.

Jesus in the Perspectives of the Latter-day Saints

The LDS Church clearly upholds many biblical beliefs about Jesus, including the historicity of his miracles, the reality of his atoning death, and the centrality of His resurrection.[1] Yet several elements in LDS christology conflict with traditional Christianity.

1. The first concerns an LDS teaching that Jesus is a created being, a notion contrary to explicit biblical teaching: Jesus proclaims "Before Abraham was I AM." (John 8:58 NKJV) Jesus is the creator of all created things, according to Colossians 1:15–17. If so, then he is uncreated, hence eternal. This same perspective undergirds the high Christology of John 1: "In the beginning was the Word, and the Word was with God, and the Word was God" (NKJV).[2]

Various LDS commentators use the word *eternal* about Jesus but not as traditional Christianity defines the word. For example, Robert Millet writes in *Bridging the Divide* that to say Jesus is eternal means that Jesus "is from one premortal existence to the next."[3] Millet is referencing the popular LDS doctrine that Jesus, like God the Father, has gone through a process of progression. In other words, Jesus is not an eternal God. There was a time, rather, when he was an eternal spirit growing into Godhood.

2. The LDS Church equates Jesus with the Jehovah of the Old Testament and makes a complete distinction between Jehovah and Elohim. Thus, contrary to historic Christianity, Elohim is a separate God from Jehovah, who, according to Mormonism, is really Jesus. This contradicts the traditional Christian interpretation that Elohim and Jehovah are names for the same God.[4]

3. The LDS Church also moves away from traditional Christology when it asserts that in his pre-earthly existence Jesus was the literal creation of God the Father and the Heavenly Mother, That creative act was sexual in nature since both God the Father and Heavenly Mother are embodied deities. While this view is not given in LDS Scripture and might not be considered official doctrine, it is the common view throughout LDS history.

4. LDS authorities have also taught that Elohim (God the Father) is the literal father of the earthly Jesus through procreation with the Virgin Mary. While not an official doctrine from one of the standard works, various LDS prophets and major LDS leaders have promoted the idea. Thus, the pre-incarnate Jesus is the product of pro-creation by Heavenly Father and Heavenly Mother while the incarnate Jesus is the product of pro-creation by Heavenly Father and Mary.

The following chart provides data on LDS understanding of the earthly birth of Jesus through Elohim (God) and the Virgin Mary.

Name of LDS figure	Elohim and Mary	Source and date
Orson Pratt	"The fleshly body of Jesus required a Mother as well as a Father. Therefore, the Father and Mother of Jesus, according to the flesh, must have been associated together in the capacity of Husband and Wife; hence the Virgin Mary must have been, for the time being, the lawful wife of God the Father."	1853, *The Seer*, vol. 1, no. 10, p. 158.
Brigham Young	"When the Virgin Mary conceived the child Jesus, the Father had begotten him in his own likeness. He was not begotten by the Holy Ghost ... it was begotten by his Father in heaven, after the same manner as the tabernacles of Cain, Abel and the rest of the sons and daughters of Adam and Eve."	1854, Journal of Discourses, 1:50
Brigham Young	"The birth of the Saviour was as natural as are the births of our children; it was the result of natural action. He partook of flesh and blood—was begotten of his Father, as we were of our fathers"	1860, Journal of Discourses, 8:115.
Joseph Fielding Smith	"Christ was begotten of God. He was not born without the aid of Man, and that Man was God!"	1954, Doctrines of Salvation 1:18, 1954, 1975
Bruce McConkie	"These name-titles all signify that our Lord is the only Son of the Father in the flesh. Each of the words is to be understood literally. Only means only; Begotten means begotten; and Son means son. Christ was begotten by an Immortal Father in the same way that mortal men are begotten by mortal fathers."	1966, Mormon Doctrine, p. 546–547

Bruce McConkie	"For our present purposes, suffice it to say that our Lord was born of a virgin, which is fitting and proper, and also natural, since the Father of the Child was an Immortal Being."	1978, The Promised Messiah, p. 466.
James Talmage	"That Child to be born of Mary was begotten of Elohim, the Eternal Father, not in violation of natural law but in accordance with a higher manifestation thereof; and, the offspring from that association of supreme sanctity, celestial Sireship, and pure though mortal maternity, was of right to be called the 'Son of the Highest.'"	1981, *Jesus the Christ*, p. 81.
Ezra Taft Benson	"The Church of Jesus Christ of Latter-day Saints proclaims that Jesus Christ is the Son of God in the most literal sense. The body in which He performed His mission in the flesh was sired by that same Holy Being we worship as God, our Eternal Father. Jesus was not the son of Joseph, nor was He begotten by the Holy Ghost. He is the Son of the Eternal Father!"	1983, *Come unto Christ*, p. 4, in *Ensign*, April 1997, p. 15.

According to LDS authorities, all humans lived in a prior state before life on earth and are, like Jesus, the literal creations of heavenly parents. More dramatically, LDS theology holds that Lucifer is also the product of the union of Father and Mother so that the pre-incarnate Jesus and Lucifer were once spiritual brothers, This idea created controversy in 2008 when Mike Huckabee raised the topic with a New York Times reporter. Huckabee was told that this was not what Mormons believed and he apologized to Mitt Romney. In actual fact, the teaching is clear in LDS history, as the following chart shows.

Name of LDS figure	Quote on Satan being Jesus' brother	Source and date
W. W. Phelps	"No wonder that Lucifer, son of the morning, the next heir to Jesus Christ, our eldest brother, should fight so hard against his brethren; he lost the glory, the honor, power, and dominion of a God and the knowledge, spirit, authority and keys of the priesthood of the son of God!"	1844, *Times and Seasons*, vol. 5, p. 758.
Joseph Fielding Smith	"We learn from the scriptures that Lucifer—once a son of the morning, who exercised authority in the presence of God before the foundations of this earth were laid—rebelled against the plan of salvation and against Jesus Christ who was chosen to be the Savior of the world and who is spoken of as the 'Lamb slain from the foundation of the world.'"	1855, Doctrines of Salvation, 2:218–19
Joseph Young	"Who is it that is at the head of this? It is the Devil, the mighty Lucifer, the great prince of the angels, and the brother of Jesus. He left the province of his Father, and took with him a third part of his Father's kingdom, and there was no other alternative but to banish him. God would have saved him if he could; but he could not."	1857, Journal of Discourses, 6:207-8.
Joseph F. Merrill	"But according to our understanding and teaching, Satan is a person with a spirit body, in form like that of all other men. He is a spirit brother of ours and of our Lord Jesus Christ, who is our Elder Brother in the spirit world."	1949, Conference Reports, April 1949, p. 27
Spencer W. Kimball	"There is another power in this world forceful and vicious. In the wilderness of Judaea, on the temple's pinnacles and on the high mountain, a momentous contest took place between two brothers, Jehovah and Lucifer, sons of Elohim."	1964, Conference Report, April 1964, p. 95

Bruce McConkie	"God lives in the family unit. He is our Father in heaven—the literal and personal Father of the spirits of all men. ... Christ was the Firstborn of all the heavenly host; Lucifer was a son of the morning: each of us came into being as conscious identities in our appointed order; and Christ is our Elder Brother."	1979, *The Mortal Messiah*, vol. 1, p. 21
Jess L. Christensen	"On first hearing, the doctrine that Lucifer and our Lord, Jesus Christ, are brothers may seem surprising to some—especially to those unacquainted with latter-day revelations. But both the scriptures and the prophets affirm that Jesus Christ and Lucifer are indeed offspring of our Heavenly Father and, therefore, spirit brothers."	1986, "I Have a Question," *Ensign*, June 1986, pp, 25–26.
LDS Primary School Teaching Manual	"1. In the premortal life we were spirit children and lived with our heavenly parents (Hebrews 12:9). 2. Jesus was the firstborn spirit child of Heavenly Father (D&C 93:21) and is the older brother of our spirits. 3. Lucifer, who became Satan, was also a spirit child of Heavenly Father."	1997, Primary 7: New Testament, Lesson 2

The Holy Spirit

The person of the Holy Spirit is not mentioned in LDS literature as much as the Father and Son. Briefly, the following points summarize current LDS teaching. Note the parallels to LDS views of the Father and Son.

1. The Holy Spirit is a separate God from the Father and the Son.

2. The Spirit is not embodied.

3. The Spirit has progressed to Godhood, like Father and Son.

4. The Holy Spirit is male, a son of the Father.

5. It is unclear whether the Holy Spirit will ever gain a body.

The LDS doctrine of the Spirit has been in flux through Mormon history. For example, in the Lectures on Faith (1835), which were originally part of Mormon scripture, the Holy Spirit is viewed as the "the mind of God" shared by Father and Son.[5] Later, LDS writers declared that the Spirit was a third person in the Godhead. There was also speculation in LDS history over whether the Spirit might be feminine or might even be Heavenly Mother, but both of those options were dismissed.[6]

Humanity and Godhood

As noted above, LDS authorities believe that humans pre-existed this earthly life and were originally spirits in the eternal realm. Humans were brought to planet earth to inherit bodies and be given opportunity to freely choose God's way of life. Though the LDS Church denies the traditional Christian doctrine of original sin, Mormons do believe that humans are fallen, sinful creatures. This sinful state leads to the question that evangelical Christians often ask, echoing the Philippian jailer: "What must I do to be saved?" (Acts 16:30)

The LDS answer both agrees with and deviates from the biblical pattern. Like mainstream Christians, Mormons believe that everyone must trust Jesus for salvation. He is the only savior for a lost humanity and his death on the cross pays for and covers human sin. Mormon leaders are placing more emphasis on the fact that salvation is by grace, a change largely due to the influence of Robert L. Millet, a leading professor at Brigham Young University and influential LDS spokesperson.[7] Millet writes in his book *Grace Works*: "The great plan of happiness is a gift. Salvation, which is exaltation, which is eternal life, is free. It is not something for which we can barter, nor is it something that may be purchased with money. Neither is it, in the strictest sense, something that can be earned."[8]

Yet four major items in LDS soteriology (doctrine of salvation) differ from traditional Christianity. One is the Mormon teaching that Jesus's experience in Gethsemane is also part of his sacrifice for sin. Although this is not taught in order to undermine Calvary's sufficiency, the emphasis on Gethsemane seems inconsistent with the Bible's main focus on the actual death of Jesus as the means of salvation.[9]

Also, in traditional Christianity's view, LDS writers are far too optimistic about humanity's potential and not concerned enough with the depth of human sin. This leads to a deficient understanding of humanity and a consequent distortion of God's relation to humanity. In spite of Millet's emphasis on grace, the LDS Church's overall emphasis on human effort leads to a works-based understanding of salvation. Granted, Protestants have sometimes overstated the biblical teaching of salvation by grace alone (Eph. 2:8–9) True faith leads to works (Eph. 2:10), and faith without works is dead (James 2). Regardless, LDS focus on obedience to the prophets, emphasis on being worthy, and doing the works of righteousness creates widespread belief that salvation is by human effort.[10] This works-righteousness comes out clearly in the rituals of the Mormon Temple endowment ceremony, as will be examined in the next chapter.

The most radical LDS view of humanity involves controversial teaching that humans can become God. This notion of deification is most famously expressed in a couplet from Lorenzo Snow, an LDS prophet from 1898 until his death in 1901. In spite of his short tenure, he uttered one of the most popular statements in LDS history: "As man is, God once was; as God is, man may become."[11] While this couplet never made it into official LDS scripture, the teaching has been part of LDS orthodoxy since the days of Joseph Smith. However, there are some signs of change, with less stress overall on the doctrine that God progresses and a softening of the rhetoric about humans becoming gods.

The change in Mormon emphasis seems to have begun with Gordon B. Hinckley, fifteenth president of the LDS and Mormon prophet from 1995 to his death in 2007. In 1997 Hinckley discussed Mormon beliefs with Don Lattin, religion editor at the *San Francisco Chronicle:*

> **Lattin:** There are some significant differences in your beliefs [and other Christian churches]. For instance, don't Mormons believe that God was once a man?
>
> **Hinckley:** I wouldn't say that. There was a little couplet coined, "As man is, God once was. As God is, man may become." Now that's more of a couplet than anything else. That gets into some pretty deep theology that we don't know very much about.

Q: So you're saying the church is still struggling to understand this?

Hinckley: Well, as God is, man may become. We believe in eternal progression. Very strongly."[12]

The following summer, Hinckley again was asked about the subject in an August 4 article in *Time* magazine: "On whether his church still holds that God the Father was once a man … [Hinckley said,] 'I don't know that we teach it. I don't know that we emphasize it … I understand the philosophical background behind it, but I don't know a lot about it, and I don't think others know a lot about it.'"[13]

Though a case can be made that Hinckley lied on the topic, Mormon philosophers and theologians continue to wrestle with these matters.[14] In the ongoing LDS discussion, there is some reluctance about discussion whether God may have failed or sinned in his progression to godhood. However, the idea that God used to be a man is a consistent teaching through LDS history. Further, LDS publications continue to teach that God was once a man. In the January 2006 *Ensign* magazine it is said that God "was once a man like us," which is a quotation from Joseph Smith in the *History of the Church*.[15] The same quotation is used in the 2011 edition of *Gospel Principles*, one of the main teaching tools of the LDS Church.[16]

On this matter, simply stating that Lorenzo Snow's famous couplet is not in Mormon scripture is a truth with little relevance as long as LDS material continues to teach the view he famously espoused. In a January 2013 dialogue between Richard Mouw, Fuller Seminary president, and Bob Millet, the famous LDS scholar, Mouw mentioned that Snow's couplet was "not canonical." He then quoted Hinckley saying it is not taught anymore. Well, Hinckley was wrong and Mouw needs to press Millet and other LDS scholars for clarification. In fact, it would be helpful if LDS General Authorities and even the current prophet himself would announce that Lorenzo Snow's couplet is false and heretical.

Recent LDS teaching on human deification is sometimes giving way to biblical language about humans becoming more like Christ and more like the Heavenly Father.[17] In spite of these changes, the LDS Church and traditional Christians continue to have enormous divide in the understanding of God as Father, Son, and Spirit. While the same words are used, there is radical difference in what it means to say that God is eternal, or that God is one, or that humans are God's creation, or that Jesus was born of the Virgin Mary.

Comparison of LDS & traditional Christian views	LDS view	Traditional Christian view
God the Father was once a man	Yes	No
The Father, Son and Spirit are three separate Gods	Yes	No
There are many Gods besides Father, Son and Spirit	Yes	No
Jesus is one in substance with God the Father	No	Yes
Jesus is eternal God in the past	No	Yes
Jesus grew up to be God in prior existence	Yes	No
In his pre-earthly existence Jesus is a product of Heavenly Father and Mother, along with Lucifer and humans	Yes	No
Jesus was conceived by the Holy Spirit through the Virgin Mary	No	Yes
Jesus was conceived through physical contact between Elohim and Mary	Yes	No

The Temple
and the Secrets

In an entry in *The Encyclopedia of Mormonism* LDS scholar Hugh Nibley states that the Mormon temple is where this world meets the next.[1] That is one indication of the importance of temples in the life of the Mormon Church and its members. For many Mormons the first visit to the temple is a high point of spiritual life because it signifies entry into a world of holy mystery. Mormons believe that Joseph Smith's task of restoring the gospel included temple building and bringing back ancient ceremonies to the one church of Jesus Christ.

There are now Mormon temples all over the world. During Smith's life Mormons built and dedicated a temple in Kirtland, Ohio. Temples were proposed for three sites in Missouri but were never completed due to the persecution and wars of the 1830s.[2] The Nauvoo temple was dedicated two years after the death of the prophet. After Brigham Young and the LDS moved to Utah, temples were dedicated in St. George (1877), Logan, (1884), Manti (1888), and Salt Lake in 1893. The Laie temple was dedicated in Hawaii in 1919.

The first Canadian temple opened in Cardston, Alberta in 1923. The first European temples were dedicated in 1955 (Bern) and 1958 (London). A New Zealand temple was also dedicated in 1958. Only one temple was dedicated in the 1960s (Oakland) while four temples were finished in the 1970s, including Washington (1974) and San Paulo (1978). Since the 1980s the prophets of the church have placed great stress on construction and use of temples all over the world, with 138 LDS temples now in operation.

Temple Basics

Mormon temples are distinct from Mormon churches. Mormon churches are found in thousands of neighbourhoods and are equivalent to Protestant or Catholic churches, used for Sunday worship and educational and administrative life of local fellowships. Mormon temples, however, are devoted solely to sacred ceremonies. Mormons who go through the ceremonies take a vow not to reveal some of the details. However, ex-Mormons provided information on the rituals from early in LDS history and there are various sources today (both in print and online) that give every word of the temple ceremonies.[3] Entrance to the Temple is restricted to Mormons who are regarded as worthy. A Temple Recommend or Pass is given by the local Mormon bishop to those who pass LDS standards involving loyalty, tithing, obedience to the authorities, and commitment to LDS morals, including the Word of Wisdom. The latter is a health-code revelation given to Joseph Smith and includes a command to abstain from tobacco, alcohol, and caffeine drinks).[4]

Mormons go through a two-fold interview process involving both general and specific items in order to gain permission to enter the temple. The following questions, from the year 2000, demonstrate the attention paid both to upholding the faith of the Mormon community, and the moral life of the individual:

1. Do you have faith in and a testimony of God the Eternal Father, His Son Jesus Christ, and the Holy Ghost?

2. Do you have a testimony of the Atonement of Christ and of His role as Savior and Redeemer?

3. Do you have a testimony of the restoration of the gospel in these the latter days?

4. Do you sustain the President of the Church of Jesus Christ of Latter-day Saints as the Prophet, Seer, and Revelator and as the only person on the earth who possesses and is authorized to exercise all priesthood keys? Do you sustain members of the First Presidency and the Quorum of the Twelve Apostles as prophets, seers, and revelators? Do you sustain the other General Authorities and local authorities of the Church?

5. Do you live the law of chastity?

6. Is there anything in your conduct relating to members of your family that is not in harmony with the teachings of the Church?

7. Do you support, affiliate with, or agree with any group or individual whose teachings or practices are contrary to or oppose those accepted by the Church of Jesus Christ of Latter-day Saints?

8. Do you strive to keep the covenants you have made, to attend your sacrament and other meetings, and to keep your life in harmony with the laws and commandments of the gospel?

9. Are you honest in your dealings with your fellowmen?

10. Are you a full-tithe payer?

11. Do your keep the Word of Wisdom?

12. Do you have financial or other obligations to a former spouse or children? If yes, are you current in meeting those obligations?

13. If you have previously received your temple endowment: Do you keep the covenants that you made in the temple? Do you wear the garment both night and day as instructed in the endowment and in accordance with the covenant you made in the temple?

14. Have there been any sins or misdeeds in your life that should have been resolved with priesthood authorities but have not been?

15. Do you consider yourself worthy to enter the Lord's house and participate in temple ordinances?

Once accepted as worthy, individuals may witness or participate in the four rituals or ordinances that take place in the temple: (1) sealing ceremonies, (2) baptism for the dead; (3) endowments for the dead and the living, and (4) second endowments or anointings.[5] The first three rituals involve ceremonies common and familiar to all of the LDS faithful. Little is known of the second anointings, unique blessings given on special occasions to select individuals.

Sealing Ceremonies

Temple sealings involve both marriage between husband and wife and the sealing of children to parents. A faithful LDS couple with a pass can get married for time (this life) and eternity. Both the marriage ceremony and the separate sealing of children to parents involve LDS belief that marriage and family life can be forever in the highest realm of heaven. As well, sealing ceremonies can be performed for both the living and the dead. For example, after Joseph Smith's death various Mormon women were sealed to him in marriage for eternity.[6] Various Mormon officials did the sealings and they included both single and married women. Sometimes the married woman's husband stood as proxy for Joseph Smith, as was the case with George Harris and his wife Lucinda in 1846.[7]

The marriage and family sealings are quite brief.

SEALER: Brother _____, do you take Sister _____ by the right hand and receive her unto yourself to be your lawfully wedded wife, for time and all eternity, with a covenant and promise that you will observe and keep all the laws, rites, and ordinances pertaining to this holy order of matrimony in the new and everlasting covenant; and this you do in the presence of God, angels, and these witnesses of your own free will and choice?

SEALER: Sister _____, do you take Brother _____ by the right hand and give yourself to him to be his lawfully wedded wife, and receive him to be your lawfully wedded husband, for time and all eternity, with a covenant and promise that you will observe and keep all the laws, rites, and ordinances pertaining to this holy order of matrimony in the new and everlasting covenant; and this you do in the presence of God, angels, and these witnesses of your own free will and choice?[8]

Baptism for the dead

Baptism for the dead is the best-known temple ceremony, possibly because of international protests when individual non-Mormons have been baptized by proxy by a LDS member. Both in 1995 and 2012 the First Presidency issued a worldwide directive that "without exception,

Church members must not submit for proxy temple ordinances any names from unauthorized groups, such as celebrities and Jewish Holocaust victims."9

The baptism ceremony is also brief. LDS members gather in the large baptismal tanks in the various temples and are baptized by immersion for deceased relatives who lacked opportunity to receive Christ. The baptismal act proceeds after this declaration by an official:

> Brother (or Sister) _____, having been commissioned of Jesus Christ, I baptize you for and in behalf of _____, who is dead, in the name of the Father, and of the Son, and of the Holy Ghost. Amen.

Baptisms for the dead take up most of the work in the temple and are the main reason for the massive genealogical research carried out by the Mormon Church. There is logic to the LDS endeavor. If proxy baptisms give the dead an opportunity to be redeemed, it is imperative to trace ancestors so that they can be redeemed.

Endowment ceremony

While baptism for the dead is the most frequent ritual, the endowment ceremony is the longest and the most symbolically powerful activity in Mormon temple life. The ceremony is an initiation rite. As the endowment ceremony begins, participants are given a new name which will be used in the afterlife. Later during the rite, they are taught the secret handclasps and signs that will be necessary to meet God after death.

Brigham Young, the second Mormon prophet, stated:

> Your endowment is to receive all those ordinances in the House of the Lord which are necessary for you, after you have departed this life, to enable you to walk back to the presence of the Father, passing the angels who stand as sentinels, being enabled to give them the key words, the signs and tokens, pertaining to the Holy Priesthood, and gain your eternal exaltation in spite of earth and hell."10

The endowment ceremony begins with washings/anointings and getting dressed in proper temple garments which includes both inner and outer clothing. After this, the participants process through a lengthy ritual that tells the story of man's fall and redemption.

The drama unfolds in five parts: Creation, Garden, Telestial, Terrestrial, and Veil. The Garden references the fall of Adam and Eve. Telestial, Terrestrial, and Veil involves the process of redemption from life on earth (Telestial) to receiving instructions to enter a higher realm (Terrestrial) and going through the Veil to the Celestial or highest realm where God dwells. The endowment ceremony is quite long and complicated.

Section	Word count
Introduction	698
Creation Total	3,237
Creation Day One	122
Creation Day Two	177
Creation Day Three	215
Creation Day Four	119
Creation Day Five	309
Creation Day Six	2291
The Laws Total	3,333
The Law of Obedience	481
The Law of Sacrifice	299
The Tokens of the Aaronic Priesthood	1,645
The First Token of the Aaronic Priesthood	684
The Lone and Dreary World: The Telestial Kingdom	1,565
The Law of the Gospel	183
The Robes of the Holy Priesthood	84
Second Token of the Aaronic Priesthood	961
The Terrestrial World	15
The Law of Chastity	121

The Tokens of the Melchizedek Priesthood or Sign of the Nail	1,221
First Token of the Melchizedek Priesthood or Sign of the Nail	756
The Law of Consecration	257
Second Token of the Melchizedek Priesthood, the Patriarchal Grip, or Sure Sign of the Nail	465
The Prayer Circle and the True Order of Prayer	730
The Veil of the Temple: Entrance to the Celestial Kingdom	1312
Ceremony at the Veil	600
Total word count	14,395

A sample text from the ceremony shows the enormous level of detail for participants to grasp as the drama unfolds.

PETER: We will now give unto you the First Token of the Melchizedek Priesthood, or the Sign of the Nail, with its accompanying name and sign. This token is received by bringing the right hand into this position: the hand vertical, the fingers close together, and the thumb extended; and the person giving the token placing the tip of the forefinger of his right hand in the center of the palm, and the thumb opposite on the back of the hand of the one receiving it, in this manner. We desire all to receive it. All arise.

(After Officiator and male witness demonstrate token at the altar, temple workers circulate around room to administer this token to the patrons.)

PETER: If any of you have not received this token, you will please raise your hand. The name of this token is "the Son", meaning the Son of God.

The sign is made by bringing the left hand in front of you with the hand in cupping shape, the left arm forming a square; the right hand is also brought forward, the palm down, the fingers close together with the thumb extended. (The Officiator makes the sign.) This is the sign.

I will now explain the covenant and obligation which are associated with this token, its name and sign and which you will be required to take upon yourselves. If I were receiving the Endowment today, either for myself or for the dead, I would repeat in my mind these words, after making the sign:

I solemnly covenant before God, angels, and these witnesses, in the name of the Son that I will never reveal the First Token of the Melchizedek Priesthood or Sign of the Nail, with its accompanying name and sign.[11]

Changes in the Endowment Ceremony

Many statements from LDS authorities say that the endowment ceremony never changes. For example, Joseph Smith said that the temple ordinances were set to be "the same forever and ever."[12] One Temple Department official stated: "some members wonder if the ordinances can be changed or adjusted. These ordinances have been provided by revelation, and are in the hands of the First Presidency. Thus, the temple is protected from tampering."[13] The impression is given from these statements and others that today's ceremonies are exactly like those in Smith's day and are comparable to ceremonies in the early Christian Church and in Old Testament days. However, Mormon leaders have introduced many changes, both minor and major, some even rooted in popular LDS desire for alterations.[14] The following table notes major changes:

Year	Change
1877	Endowments for the dead added
1919–1927	Oath of vengeance removed
1919–1927	Language about graphic penalties removed
1923	Shorter endowment garment approved for outside use
1970s	Reference to Satan having black skin is dropped
1978	Blacks are now allowed to participate in Temple ceremonies
1990	All penalties removed from vows

1990	Wives no longer have to take vow of obedience to husband
1990	Text about Lucifer's preacher removed
1990	Five points of fellowship taken out of endowment
1990	The phrase "pay lay ale" is dropped
1990	Eve is no longer faulted for the Fall
2005	Participants clothe themselves
2005	Washing and anointing is on head only

The changes arose because of concerns of the LDS leadership and the larger LDS community. Some of the revisions simply reflect changing mores and attitudes among LDS members and increasing sensitivities to the non-LDS world. Some changes have to do with increased concern for modesty. In Utah in the late 1800s washings were performed while naked in a big tub, with men and women in separate rooms. The bathing would be in private but the tub washings stopped sometime in the twentieth century. Until 2005, the washings and anointings involved touching various parts of the body, but since 2005 the washings and anointings involve touching only the head. Further, the garment now worn during initial washings and anointings is much more modest than in the past.

Some oaths have been removed. The oath of vengeance (dropped in 1927) involved LDS commitment to punish the United States for the killing of Joseph and his brother Hyrum. Endowment participants were told: "You and each of you do covenant and promise that you will pray and never cease to pray to Almighty God to avenge the blood of the prophets upon this nation, and that you will teach the same to your children and to your children's children unto the third and fourth generation." The oath received scrutiny when Mormon Apostle Reed Smoot was elected to the US Senate in 1903.

In the 1920s LDS leaders also urged the removal of graphic language related to penalties if one revealed the secrets of the two priesthoods. Here is the oath related to the first priesthood as it would have been said in the early 1920s: "We, and each of us, covenant and promise that we will not reveal any of the secrets of this, the first token of the Aaronic priesthood, with its accompanying name, sign or penalty. Should we do so; *we agree that our throats be cut from ear to ear and our tongues torn out by their roots.*" Sometime after 1931 the harsh wording was removed though hand signs were used to indicate the penalties. Through most of the twentieth century participants vowed never to reveal the secrets and stated: "Rather than do so, I would suffer my life to be taken." After 1990 even this wording was taken out.[15]

In 1990 LDS authorities dropped a dialogue involving Lucifer, various biblical figures, and a Christian pastor. Here is part of the narrative from the pre-1990 ceremony.

(Re-enter Lucifer)

Lucifer—"I hear you. What is it you want?"

Adam—"Who are you?"

Lucifer—"The god of this world."

Adam—"Who made you the god of this world?"

Lucifer—"I made myself. What is it that you want?"

Adam—"I was calling on Father."

Lucifer—"Oh, I see, you want religion. I'll have some preachers along presently."

(Enter Preacher)

Preacher—"You have a very fine congregation here."

Lucifer—"Oh, are you a Preacher?"

Preacher—"Yes."

Lucifer—"Ever been to college and studied the dead languages?"

Preacher—"Why, certainly; no one can preach the gospel acceptably unless he has been to college and studied the dead languages."

Lucifer—"Well, if you'll preach your gospel to this congregation and convert them, mind you, I'll give you—let me see—four thousand a year."

Preacher—"That is very little, but I'll do the best I can."

Preacher *(To Adam)*—"Good morning, sir."

Adam—"Good morning."

Preacher—"I understand you are looking for religion?"

Adam—"I was calling upon Father."

Preacher *(To Adam)*—"Do you believe in that great Spirit, without body, parts or passions, who sits on the top of a topless
throne, 'beyond the bounds of time and space', whose center is
everywhere and circumference nowhere; who fills immensity
with His presence and yet is so small He can dwell in your
heart. Do you believe this?"
Adam—"No. I don't believe a word of it."[16]

Masonic Connections and Theological Concerns

Where did Joseph Smith get the signs and wording related to the
priesthood and other parts of the endowment? Most Mormons would
contend that Smith received endowment rituals through direct revelation. However, the first Mormons knew that a lot of the material came
from Smith's involvement in the Masonic lodge. He became a Mason
in 1842 and shortly after imported elements of Masonry into the temple rituals. Mike Homer and other scholars have provided abundant
documentation of the link between Masonic ritual and the temple
endowment ceremony.[17] Early Mormons believed that Smith took the
best of the lodge ritual and through revelation provided the Latter-day
community with a restored and fuller ceremony.

Two caveats are in order concerning the Masonic connection. First,
most of the endowment ceremony involves LDS doctrine that has little
to do with Lodge teaching. The connections to Masonic ritual are
clear, but should not be overstated. Second, Mormons have never
enforced the penalties connected to breaking the vows literally. There
are no records of people killing themselves or being killed because the
secrets were revealed. The harsh penalties invoked are a symbolic way
of suggesting the importance of the vow of silence.

Three major theological issues must be faced in consideration of the
Mormon temple rituals. First, what do secret handclasps, names, and garments have to do with the plain Gospel revealed in the New Testament?
There are no temple ceremonies in the early Church and none throughout church history. Do Mormons not know that the Masonic rites only
date back to the late seventeenth and early eighteenth centuries?

Second, it is tragic that the endowment ceremony and the whole
process of a temple recommend enforce the notion that salvation for
the LDS involves works righteousness. In the New Testament salvation

is by grace. There is absolutely no mention of temple recommends or secret handshakes or secret vows in the gospel of Jesus. Entering the heavenly kingdom does not hinge on remembering your secret temple name. It is quite telling that the word grace appears only once in the endowment ceremony while the word law appears 44 times.

The endowment ceremony offers proof that the LDS understanding of soteriology or salvation is too distant from the simplicity of the Gospel of the New Testament. The ceremony ties in with the convoluted plan of eternal progression taught by LDS authorities. This plan tracks the human from existence as intelligence in the eternal past to possible godhood in the highest of the three heavens, as shown in the following chart.

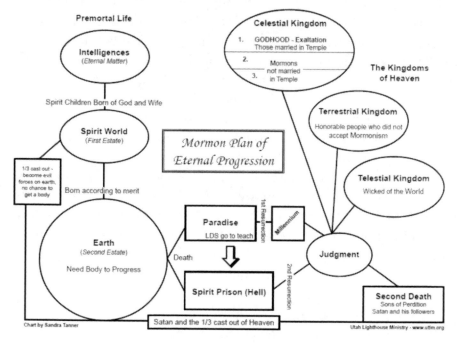

Finally, the endowment ceremony shows a lack of focus on Jesus.[18] While there are some references to Jesus, his presence is rather muted and there is no clear and sustained focus on the message of his life, death, and resurrection. This is a tragedy. The Mormon prophets have given their blessing to a ceremony which puts more attention on proper handshakes and secret names than on the person and work of Jesus Christ. Again, it is quite telling that the name Jesus appears only nine times in the text while the archangel Michael is mentioned 32 times.

Blacks and the Priesthood

On June 8, 1978 the First Presidency of the LDS Church announced a lifting of the ban against blacks holding the priesthood. Prophet Spencer W. Kimball said that he received a revelation from God on the matter after spending time in prayer and meditation in the Salt Lake Temple. The revelation was approved by the Quorum of the Twelve Apostles and then by the General Conference on September 30, 1978. The main part of the June announcement states the following:

> Aware of the promises made by the prophets and presidents of the Church who have preceded us that at some time, in God's eternal plan, all of our brethren who are worthy may receive the priesthood, and witnessing the faithfulness of those from whom the priesthood has been withheld, we have pleaded long and earnestly in behalf of these, our faithful brethren, spending many hours in the Upper Room of the Temple supplicating the Lord for divine guidance.
>
> He has heard our prayers, and by revelation has confirmed that the long-promised day has come when every faithful, worthy man in the Church may receive the holy priesthood, with power to exercise its divine authority, and enjoy with his loved ones every blessing that flows therefrom, including the blessings of the temple. Accordingly, all worthy male members of the Church may be ordained to the priesthood without regard for race or color.[1]

The revelation to Prophet Kimball brought a closure on this topic for most LDS.[2] The current position of Church leadership is clear, as shown in the Statement on "Race and the Church: All Are Alike Unto God" released on February 29, 2012.

The Church unequivocally condemns racism, including any and all past racism by individuals both inside and outside the Church. In 2006, then Church president Gordon B. Hinckley declared that "no man who makes disparaging remarks concerning those of another race can consider himself a true disciple of Christ. Nor can he consider himself to be in harmony with the teachings of the Church. Let us all recognize that each of us is a son or daughter of our Father in Heaven, who loves all of His children."[3]

The day prior to the Statement BYU Professor Randy Bott made controversial remarks in a *Washington Post* article.[4] According to the Post reporter, Bott defended various elements of the historic LDS position on blacks. What makes the Bott controversy rather complicated is that he was repeating explanations for the priesthood restriction that became standard among LDS leaders over the previous century and a half.[5] The following points represent the LDS position on race by the end of the 19th century, an outlook that lasted until the policy change in 1978.

1. Black skin is a sign of a divine curse.
2. Blacks descend from Cain, the son of Adam and Eve, and Ham, one of the sons of Noah. Both Cain and Ham were cursed for their disobedience to God.[6]
3. Birth on earth with black skin relates to failure in pre-mortal existence.
4. Blacks cannot hold the priesthood.

After the Washington Post article the LDS Church responded by declaring that Bott's positions "absolutely do not represent the teachings and doctrines of The Church of Jesus Christ of latter-day Saints." After noting the past restriction on priesthood for blacks, the Statement claims that "it is not known precisely why, how, or when this restriction began in the church but what is clear is that it ended decades ago. Some have attempted to explain the reason for this restriction but these attempts should be viewed as speculation and opinion, not doctrine."

Bott's views created enormous controversy. He apologized for the confusion created by the article but said he was misquoted. Various analysts pointed out that the *Washington Post* article was consistent with Bott's prior blog postings on the issue of race.[7]

Obviously, past LDS racism is rooted in the larger racist element in nineteenth century America and in some of its churches.[8] Various denominations have expressed regret for past racism. While the LDS Church has repudiated racism there has been no official apology for statements by previous prophets and apostles that condoned racist views, including second Mormon prophet Brigham Young.[9]

As well, the LDS situation is complicated by racist overtones in Mormon scriptures. For example, 2 Nephi 5:21 in the Book of Mormon states this about a curse on the Lamanites: "For behold, they had hardened their hearts against him, that they had become like unto a flint; wherefore, as they were white, and exceedingly fair and delightsome, that they might not be enticing unto my people the Lord God did cause a skin of blackness to come upon them." The Book of Moses claims that "the Lord shall curse the land with much heat, and the barrenness thereof shall go forth forever; and there was a blackness came upon all the children of Canaan, that they were despised among all people." (7:8)

There is debate to what extent racist views can be traced back to Joseph Smith. Lester Bush, Newell Bringhurst, and Armand Mauss have done significant work on the history of racist views in LDS history. Their research confirms the following:

1. Joseph Smith had an ambivalent view about the abolition of slavery. Some of his writings opposed the abolitionists while other writings adopt a gradualist view towards ending slavery.

2. Smith made no official statement banning blacks from the priesthood.

3. Elijah Abel, a black member, entered the priesthood in 1836. Joseph Smith attended his ordination.[10] During Smith's lifetime other blacks gained the priesthood.

4. Some early Mormon leaders used statements in the Book of Moses and the Book of Abraham to argue that black skin was a curse related to descent from Ham and Cain.

5. The most explicit bans against blacks holding the priesthood begin in 1847. By 1900 the Mormon community assumed this ban could be traced back to Joseph Smith.

Of course, even if Smith was not opposed to blacks holding the priesthood, what can be said about the LDS prophets from Brigham Young on who upheld the ban? If racism is clearly wrong, why did Prophet Kimball have to pray to have the ban lifted? Did God approve racism from 1847 to 1978 and then change His mind? A proper estimate of LDS prophets and apostles must pay attention to the racist element of the past, combined, of course, with acknowledgement of the lifting of the ban in 1978 and the increasingly clear repudiation of racism since then.

What is most needed, of course, is an admission from the LDS leadership that the ban itself was wrong since it was based on a racist perspective. Further, full resolution on racism will not be reached until LDS leaders recognize and condemn racist elements in Mormon scripture, as noted above. As well, LDS leaders need to explicitly acknowledge that previous Mormon prophets have been racist in their teachings. This applies especially to Brigham Young.

What is especially galling in recent LDS Statements on Racism is that Church leaders have no problem in condemning Randy Bott by name for his explanations about past racism while these same leaders lack the courage to name past LDS prophets by name who actually created and advanced the racist theories that dominated in LDS history.

Leader	Quote	Source and date
Brigham Young	"Shall I tell you the law of God in regard to the African race? If the white man who belongs to the chosen seed mixes his blood with the seed of Cain, the penalty, under the law of God, is death on the spot. This will always be so."	Journal of Discourses, Volume 10, page 110.
Brigham Young	"You see some classes of the human family that are black, uncouth, un- comely, disagreeable and low in their habits, wild, and seemingly deprived of nearly all the blessings of the intelligence that is generally bestowed upon mankind... Cain might have been killed, and that would have put a termination to that line of human beings. This was not to be, and the Lord put a mark upon him, which is the flat nose and black skin."	Journal of Discourses 7:290-291, October 9, 1859.

Brigham Young	"You may inquire of the intelligent of the world whether they can tell why the aborigines of this country are dark, loathsome, ignorant, and sunken into the depths of degradation... if they transgress [the Lord's] law, change his ordinances, and break his covenants he has made with them, he will put a mark upon them... but by-and-by they will become a white and delightsome people"	Journal of Discourses 7:336
Brigham Young	Trace mankind down to after the flood, and then another curse is pronounced upon the same race - that they should be the "servant of servants;" and they will be, until that curse is removed; and the Abolitionists cannot help it, nor in the least alter that decree.	Journal of Discourses 7:290-291, October 9, 1859
John Taylor	"And after the flood we are told that the curse that had been pronounced upon Cain was continued through Ham's wife, as he had married a wife of that seed. And why did it pass through the flood? Because it was necessary that the devil should have a representation upon the earth as well as God."	Journal of Discourses, Vol. 22, page 304
Joseph Fielding Smith	"Millions of souls have come into this world cursed with a black skin and have been denied the privilege of Priesthood and the fullness of the blessings of the Gospel. These are the descendants of Cain... we will also hope that blessings may eventually be given to our negro brethren, for they are our brethren—children of God—not withstanding their black covering emblematical of eternal darkness."	The Way to Perfection, pages 101-102.

Joseph Fielding Smith	"There is a reason why one man is born black and with other disadvantages, while another is born white with great advantages... Those who were faithful in all things there received greater blessings here, and those who were not faithful received less."	Doctrines of Salvation, p. 61
Joseph Fielding Smith	"I would not want you to believe that we bear any animosity toward the Negro. "Darkies" are wonderful people, and they have their place in our church."	Look magazine, October 22, 1963, page 79.
Joseph Fielding Smith	"President Brigham Young... said that Joseph Smith had declared that the Negroes were not neutral in heaven, for all the spirits took sides, but the posterity of Cain are black because he (Cain) committed murder."	The Way to Perfection, pages 105-106.
Joseph Fielding Smith	"That negro race, for instance, have been placed under restrictions because of their attitude in the world of spirits, few will doubt. It cannot be looked upon as just that they should be deprived of the power of the Priesthood without it being a punishment for some act, or acts, performed before they were born."	The Way to Perfection, page 43.
Joseph Fielding Smith	"Ham, through Egyptus, continued the curse which was placed upon the seed of Cain. Because of that curse this dark race was separated and isolated from all the rest of Adam's posterity before the flood, and since that time the same condition has continued, and they have been 'despised among all people.' This doctrine did not originate with President Brigham Young but was taught by the Prophet Joseph Smith .... we all know it is due to his teachings that the negro today is barred from the Priesthood."	The Way to Perfection, pages 110-111.

Official Statement	"The attitude of the Church with reference to Negroes remains as it has always stood. It is not a matter of the declaration of a policy but of direct commandment from the Lord, on which is founded the doctrine of the Church from the days of its organization, to the effect that Negroes may become members of the Church but that they are not entitled to the priesthood at the present time."	August 17, 1949 The First Presidency
Spencer W. Kimball	"The day of the Lamanites in nigh. For years they have been growing delightsome... The children in the home placement program in Utah are often lighter than their brothers and sisters... These young members of the Church are changing to whiteness and to delightsomeness."	Spencer W. Kimball in The Improvement, Era, Dec. 1960, p. 923
Apostle Bruce R. McConkie	"Negroes in this life are denied the Priesthood; under no circumstances can they hold this delegation of authority from the Almighty. (Abra. 1:20-27.)"	Mormon Doctrine, 1966, pp. 527-528
Apostle Mark E. Petersen	"The reason that one would lose his blessings by marrying a Negro is due to the restriction placed upon them. "No person having the least particle of Negro blood can hold the Priesthood" (Brigham Young). It does not matter if they are one-sixth Negro or one-hundred and sixth, the curse of no Priesthood is the same."	
Apostle Mark E. Petersen	"The discussion on civil rights, especially over the last 20 years, has drawn some very sharp lines...We who teach in the Church certainly must have our feet on the ground and not to be led astray by the philosophies of men on this subject..."	

Apostle Mark E. Petersen	"I think I have read enough to give you an idea of what the Negro is after. He is not just seeking the opportunity of sitting down in a cafe where white people eat. He isn't just trying to ride on the same streetcar or the same Pullman car with white people... the Negro seeks absorption with the white race. He will not be satisfied until he achieves it by intermarriage."
Apostle Mark E. Petersen	"Was segregation a wrong principle? ... When he told Enoch not preach the gospel to the descendants of Cain who were black, the Lord engaged in segregation. When He cursed the descendants of Cain as to the Priesthood, He engaged in segregation..."
Apostle Mark E. Petersen	"Who placed the Negroes originally in darkest Africa? Was it some man, or was it God? And when He placed them there, He segregated them..."
Apostle Mark E. Petersen	"The Lord segregated the people both as to blood and place of residence. At least in the cases of the Lamanites and the Negro we have the definite word of the Lord Himself that he placed a dark skin upon them as a curse—as a punishment and as a sign to all others. He forbade intermarriage with them under threat of extension of the curse."
Apostle Mark E. Petersen	"Now we are generous with the Negro. We are willing that the Negro have the highest education. I would be willing to let every Negro drive a Cadillac if they could afford it. I would be willing that they have all the advantages they can get out of life in the world. But let them enjoy these things among themselves... what God hath separated, let not man bring together again."

Apostle Mark E. Petersen	"In spite of all he did in the pre-existent life, the Lord is willing, if the Negro accepts the gospel with real, sincere faith, and is really converted, to give him the blessings of baptism and the gift of the Holy Ghost. If that Negro is faithful all his days, he can and will enter the celestial kingdom. He will go there as a servant, but he will get celestial glory."	Race Problems - As They Affect The Church, Convention of Teachers of Religion on the College Level, Brigham Young University, Provo, Utah, August 27, 1954
Letter to all general and local priesthood officers of The Church of Jesus Christ of Latter-day Saints throughout the world	"He has heard our prayers, and by revelation has confirmed that the long-promised day has come when every faithful, worthy man in the Church may receive the holy priesthood, with power to exercise its divine authority, and enjoy with his loved ones every blessing that flows therefrom, including the blessings of the temple. Accordingly, all worthy male members of the Church may be ordained to the priesthood without regard for race or color."	June 8, 1978

Conclusions

In order to make some general observations about a way forward for the Church of Jesus Christ of Latter-day Saints, it is helpful to outline the major points reached in the preceding chapters. The list below follows the order of presentation in this book.

1. The 1838 First Vision account is a late fabrication of Joseph Smith.
2. There is no reliable evidence for visitation of the embodied Father and Son to Joseph in 1820.
3. The First Vision accounts contradict one another.
4. There was no total apostasy in the Christian Church shortly after the New Testament period.
5. Joseph Smith engaged in the fraudulent, superstitious, and criminal practice of money digging.
6. Joseph Smith was arrested and fined in relation to money digging.
7. Joseph Smith used the same seer stone in translating the Book of Mormon as he did for his money digging.
8. Joseph Smith broke his wedding vows.
9. Joseph Smith treated his wife in an abusive way over celestial marriage.[1]
10. Joseph Smith coerced women to marry him.
11. Joseph Smith lied repeatedly over years about his plural wives.
12. Joseph Smith pressured other Mormons to lie about polygamy.

13. Joseph Smith coerced young women to marry him, including two who were his guardians.
14. Joseph Smith pressured already married women to marry him.
15. Joseph Smith made false prophecies about the return of Christ.
16. Joseph Smith made false prophecies about gaining wealth in Salem.
17. Joseph Smith made false prophecies about his Kirtland bank's success.
18. Joseph Smith made false prophecies about the success of the LDS in Missouri.[2]
19. Joseph Smith (and Sidney Rigdon) fomented the conflicts in Missouri.[3]
20. Joseph Smith altered his own revelations.
21. Joseph Smith fabricated the revelation on priesthood restoration in Doctrine and Covenants section 27.
22. Joseph Smith's translation of Scripture is biased, unlearned and contrary to the earliest and best Hebrew and Greek manuscripts.
23. Mormon prophets have taught various major heresies throughout LDS history.
24. Brigham Young taught the heretical view that Adam was God.
25. Brigham Young taught the false doctrine of Blood Atonement.
26. Brigham Young and other prophets often engaged in careless speculation and advanced erroneous views like claiming there were people living on the sun or that the earth has a spirit and needs baptized.
27. Brigham Young was responsible in part for creating the environment that led to the Mountain Meadows Massacre.
28. Brigham Young lied repeatedly about the Massacre.
29. LDS Church leaders engaged in cover-up of the Massacre throughout history.
30. LDS leaders have often misled Mormons through cover-up, obfuscation, and lies about various topics.

31. Ezra Taft Benson taught a dangerous, extreme and false view about the status of the LDS prophet.

32. LDS Church members are naïve and gullible because of their unwarranted adulation of Church prophets and apostles.

33. Loyalty to God is not to be measured explicitly by obedience to the LDS authorities.

34. The Book of Mormon was written by Joseph Smith, with the help of others. It is not an ancient document.

35. The Book of Mormon is not a reliable historical account in relation to Central and North America.

36. DNA evidence about Natives contradicts the dominant view in LDS history that the Indians were originally Jewish tribes.

37. The Book of Mormon text was altered, occasionally in significant ways, after the first edition was published.

38. The teaching on God in The Book of Mormon was basically repudiated by Joseph Smith later in his life.

39. The revelations given in the 1833 Book of Commandments were sometimes altered in significant ways when they were reproduced in the 1835 Doctrine and Covenants.

40. LDS leaders tampered with LDS Scripture by removing the Lectures on Faith from the LDS canon of scripture.

41. The Book of Abraham was written by Joseph Smith.

42. The Book of Abraham is neither a regular translation nor an "inspired" translation of ancient Egyptian documents.

43. LDS doctrine that arises from the Book of Abraham is basically rooted in a document invented by Joseph and passed off to LDS members from his uninformed, naïve and false translation work on the papyrus.

44. The Book of Abraham contains a wild, irrational and unscientific cosmology, rooted in Joseph Smith's imagination and nineteenth century views.[4]

45. The LDS prophets have been wrong to teach there is more than one God.

46. The LDS prophets have been wrong to teach God the Father is not eternal and used to be a man.

47. The LDS prophets are wrong to teach that humans can become God.

48. Prophet Gordon Hinckley misled the public about the theory that God was once a man. He engaged in obfuscation with the media and then smoothed things over with the LDS membership through his General Conference remarks.

49. The truth that there is one God is a total repudiation of LDS teaching that humans can become God.

50. LDS prophets have been wrong to teach that Jesus went through a path of eternal progression.

51. LDS prophets have been wrong to teach that Jesus is the product of sex between Elohim and the Virgin Mary.

52. LDS prophets are wrong to teach that Jesus and Lucifer are spiritual brothers.

53. LDS leaders and Mitt Romney were wrong to engage in obfuscation when Mike Huckabee said that Mormons believe Jesus and Lucifer are spiritual brothers.

54. The Temple endowment ceremony is an invention of Joseph Smith.[5]

55. The Temple endowment ceremony has some of its roots in the Masonic lodge. Masonic ceremonies go back to the seventeenth century and not to the time of Solomon.

56. The Temple endowment ceremony has been altered by LDS prophets even though they claim it is the same ceremony throughout history.

57. The Temple endowment ceremony minimizes salvation by grace.

58. The LDS Church system and theology creates a works-righteousness.

59. Secret oaths and secret signs of the priesthood are totally foreign to the New Testament.

60. Wearing special temple garments is foreign to the New Testament.

61. The LDS prophets are wrong to support LDS scripture that contain racist statements.

62. The LDS prophets were wrong for decades to support racist theories.
63. LDS leaders continue to engage in obfuscation on racism in order to hide the fact that various LDS prophets have been racist in their teaching.
64. LDS leaders lied repeatedly about polygamy after the 1890 Manifesto.
65. LDS leaders were and are wrong to link polygamy to exaltation.

How will LDS prophets, scholars, and members react to this list and, more important, to the evidence and proof for these various points? If the past and present is any indication, the most likely scenario is as follows:

- The leaders at the very top of the Church will continue to ignore most if not all issues.[6]
- Some LDS scholars will admit that some of the concerns are valid, true, and right. Few of these scholars will do much to help their own prophets face reality.[7]
- Other LDS scholars will engage in cheap and misleading apologetics in order to avoid any truly honest interaction with problems, lies, cover-ups, false teachings, etc.
- The LDS public relations machine will continue to engage in obfuscation and deception in dealing with the lies, errors, false teachings, massive problems, etc.
- Most LDS members will avoid any serious engagement with the issues.

Three major realities explain why LDS members do not usually truly engage issues. The first has to do with the instant and constant reinforcement of faith through focus on subjective feelings ("burning in the bosom") and "knowledge" from the Holy Spirit that Joseph Smith is a prophet of God, the Book of Mormon is the word of God, Thomas Monson is a prophet of God, and the LDS Church is the one true Church. Millions of LDS would respond to all of the above concerns by stating: "It does not matter what you say or write since I **know** my Church is true."[8]

As noted earlier, the uncritical adulation and highly subjective affirmation of LDS leadership by rank and file members leads to isolation and insulation from the realities at the top of the Church. Most LDS members would not even know of reports that skepticism about the Book of Mormon and other basics of Mormonism extend to some members in the top levels of the Church.[9]

The LDS Church will remain in crisis as long as subjective faith in falsehood continues. A "burning in the bosom" feeling that Mormonism is true does not outweigh all the evidence that many LDS views are untrue, and that the Mormon prophets are often false teachers. Ignoring deception, immorality, and lies by LDS leaders is no mark of Christian faith. It is rather the typical reality in false religion.

The second reason most LDS members will not face all of the evidence against the basic integrity of Mormonism is simply the realization of the cost of leaving the LDS Church. It is impossible for many Mormons to even imagine walking away from the security of Mormon culture and the love they experience in the LDS Church.[10] As well, ex-Mormon testimonies are replete with stories of the price endured in family break-up, dissolution of friendships, and even business loss upon resigning, dismissal, or excommunication.

Third, there is the fear factor that underlies questions like: "What if the LDS Church is the only Church that holds the keys to the priesthood?" "What if Joseph Smith really did restore the Gospel?" These questions, of course, are legitimate but the only way to deal with them is to answer them in complete and courageous fashion. Using these questions in a rhetorical way to avoid answering them is shallow and dishonest.

The Mormon Church is in crisis. What should be recommended for improvements and for the on-going evangelical Christian and Mormon dialogue? Since the LDS Church is not going away, one should pray that LDS leaders continue to emphasize that God is eternal, teach more clearly that real spiritual growth has nothing to do with becoming God, and continue to put more focus on the person and work of Jesus Christ and salvation by grace.[11] As well, traditional Christians should pray that the LDS leaders in Salt Lake City will formally repudiate their false teaching that the Church of Jesus Christ of Latter-day Saints is the only true Church.[12] Sadly, many LDS members who come to realize that much in the LDS Church is false are often unwilling to turn to the Christian faith that is presented in the New Testament. Thereby, they miss the great case that can be made for the greatness, uniqueness and integrity of Jesus Christ.[13]

Getting to that full New Testament vision is, of course, what evangelical Christians want for Mormons. This involves the reality that the prophets of the Church should drop the secret vows and secret rituals in the Temple. If the endowment ceremony is kept it should be radically altered so that it gives no impression of earning one's way to the celestial glory by remembering your secret name or your secret handshakes. The endowment could be a beautiful ceremony if it was centered in the details of the person and work of Jesus Christ and all that he has done at Calvary to cover sin and offer eternal life.[14] The ceremony should not end with whispers about one's new name upon entering the veil but rather with a celebration of the resurrection of Jesus and his role as the one who leads us through the veil into eternity.

Temple baptism and sealing for the dead should be dropped. One obscure verse in 1 Corinthians 15 is not enough to warrant the massive program to reclaim the spirits of the deceased. LDS compassion for those who never heard the Gospel is worthy of praise but the genealogical records will never be complete. Likewise, there are not enough Temple Mormons to reach those who never got a chance to hear the gospel. This whole issue is better left to God's mercy and judgment.

Generally speaking, the LDS Church can keep much of the theology of the Book of Mormon. It is time, however, for honest LDS scholars to help their prophets get realistic about the Book of Mormon being a product of the 19th century.[15] It is even more obvious that LDS scholars need to help their General Authorities scrap the Book of Abraham entirely, especially since it contains texts that were used to support racist theories.[16] As well, the Book of Moses and the Inspired Translation of Joseph Smith should be recognized as roadblocks to accurate knowledge related to the Old and New Testament.

Doctrine and Covenants contains some theology consistent with the Bible. However, it cannot be trusted as Scripture from God since it is largely nothing more than the projections of Joseph Smith. All of the above obviously leads to the most important but difficult move that is crucial to the spiritual growth and health of the Church of Jesus Christ of Latter-day Saints.

Though it will be agonizing, current LDS prophets, leaders, and scholars need to face the obvious evidence that Joseph Smith was largely a failure as a prophet of God. He did not restore the Gospel to the earth. Rather, Smith invented a golden Bible that is unhistorical. Shortly after the launch of the Book of Mormon he broke his own wedding vows through his adultery with Fanny Alger. Later, through his lies, manipulations and coercion he foisted his polygamous and polyandrous schemes on various Mormon women.

His oversized ego led him during his late years as prophet to advance ridiculous views about God, exaltation, and salvation.[17] His boasting about doing more than Jesus speaks for itself, as do his false prophecies and careless pronouncements in his sermons. Sadly, uncritical acceptance of his prophetic status led his followers to financial ruin in Ohio, injury and death in Missouri and ultimate expulsion from Nauvoo.[18] Smith's own tragic death is not one of a martyr for Jesus but of a "rough stone rolling" arrested for criminal actions.

On most days, Smith could be the epitome of friendliness and zest for life. However, his likeable personality and his zeal in advancing his cause must not blind LDS leaders and scholars to his less worthy characteristics. LDS leaders need to remember that teachers are to be judged with greater strictness (James 3:1). The coddling of Joseph Smith and the constant rationalizations for his crimes, lies, false teachings, and immorality is especially galling in light of the strict demands made on members today.

I predict that future scholarship will do little to enhance Smith's credibility. As my work on this book was coming to an end, I learned of current research by Joseph Johnstun, a historian in Illinois. Johnstun, a Latter-day Saint, claims that his investigations strongly suggest that Smith was engaged in counterfeiting money while he led the Saints in Ohio and Illinois. While it is impossible to read Joseph Smith's mind, Johnstun's investigation is also providing further evidence that Smith had no problem in crushing members who dared to question him. Johnstun believes that Smith had various followers poisoned for their dissent against his wishes.[19]

Mormon leaders have often said that that the Church of Jesus Christ of Latter-day Saints rises or falls on the integrity of Joseph Smith. If that is the only factor in deciding things, the Church deserves to fall.

One can hope, however, that LDS leaders will have the courage to move beyond forcing a binary decision about Joseph Smith. Instead, they can keep on duplicating everything in his life and teaching that was great and be honest about his dark side that led both him and his movement into major error and failure.[20] The same strategy should be adopted for all Mormon prophets, past and present. Following this path will be difficult but Mormons have always believed in the God who can make all things new.[21]

The crisis in the LDS Church is not going to cause a total collapse. There are simply too many Mormons for that to happen. However, the crisis is not going to go away until the LDS leaders and scholars address the major blunders in LDS belief and practice, particularly those that go back to Brigham Young and especially Joseph Smith. Continuing to avoid issues or offer lame rationalizations for significant evils and false teachings related to Smith and Young will not suffice.

LDS prophets since Joseph Smith have built a façade around him. The delusions and illusions about him in the LDS worldview need to be destroyed in order to give way to historical reality, true morality, and authentic spirituality. Otherwise, LDS people are left with fables about the American natives, fraud about Egyptian documents, lies about polygamy, confusion on the Godhead, distortions about Masons and the endowment, a system of works righteousness, a minimizing of Jesus Christ, and cover-ups about racism.

This book has offered serious critique of Mormonism because there is a real crisis in the LDS Church. This crisis is not caused by ex-Mormons like Sandra Tanner or Grant Palmer or others. Rather, the crisis is self-induced by core failings in the religion itself, in its founder, and in later prophets. In 1836 when Joseph Smith's false prophecies and careless banking procedures created mass exodus from the LDS Church, Smith ran away. LDS leaders today should not duplicate him in facing their own Mormon moment and its crisis.

Postscript

This book was going to print just as the LDS Church announced a new digital and print edition of the English scriptures (the Holy Bible, Book of Mormon, Doctrine and Covenants and Pearl of Great Price). The introduction to the Book of Abraham is now said to be "an inspired translation of the writings of Abraham." The addition of the word "inspired" probably indicates awareness that it is not a translation in the regular meaning of the word. The way the introduction reads in this new edition also indicates a distancing between the "inspired translation" and the Egyptian papyrus. The new edition states that "Joseph Smith began the translation in 1835 after obtaining some Egyptian papyri." In spite of these changes the heading to the actual text of the Book of Abraham remains the same, asserting that it is "a Translation of some ancient Records that have fallen into our hands from the catacombs of Egypt."

The Conclusions to *Mormon Crisis* contain frequent comments about lack of straightforward language from LDS leaders and scholars. This postscript gives space for three more examples. Various top scholars in the LDS Church have given me opposing opinion on whether the Church still stands by the view that God used to be a man. This divide came up as early as 2004 when I covered the Ravi Zacharias sermon in the Salt Lake Tabernacle. Some Mormon leaders told me the LDS Church was moving away from the traditional LDS view. However, some LDS missionaries fresh from their training told me the opposite view when we talked at the Salt Lake airport on our way out of town. The First Presidency should settle this issue once and for all.

Larry McMurtry noticed the same kind of fuzziness when he dealt with criticism over his controversial piece on Richard Bushman's *Rough Stone Rolling* in the *New York Review of Books* (November 17, 2005). In a follow-up letter McMurtry asserted that he had read all of Bushman and prefers Fawn Brodie's biography on Joseph Smith. McMurtry states: "She saw the fraud at the heart of Mormonism and she describes it. Professor Bushman pitty-pats around it." McMurtry concludes his letter by noting the Mountain Meadows Massacre and states: "Should the Mormon leadership ever work up to admitting the truth about Mountain Meadows, then Mormonism might be considered an ethical faith: but not before." (Letter to the editor, NYRB, March 23, 2006).

The third case involves contemporary LDS affirmation of monotheism. Two questions arise for further reflection. First, if contemporary LDS leaders believe in only one God, can they declare that Joseph Smith is totally wrong to proclaim belief in many Gods? Second, would it not be appropriate to remove the hymn "Praise to the Man" from the current LDS hymnbook since it refers to Smith "mingling with Gods" after his ascension?

Careful readers will note that I have not questioned the motives of any current LDS leaders or scholars, even though criticism has been given strongly on lack of clarity, duplicity, etc. Weaknesses in these areas are not necessarily proof of bad motives. In relation to whether Mormonism is Christian, the following would represent my viewpoint.

The Church of Jesus Christ of Latter-day Saints is **not** the "only true Church." Many major aspects of former and current LDS belief are not consistent with the true, authentic Christian faith and beliefs of the church founded by Jesus. These elements are so serious that Mormonism must be referred to as sub-Christian, anti-Christian or non-Christian at those points. Obviously, Mormonism contains true Christian elements but this is no excuse for LDS leaders and scholars to ignore the very serious theological, ethical and spiritual errors and problems at the heart of much of LDS faith.

The concerns I have expressed in this book are **not** meant to be read in any way as judgment about the ultimate spiritual state of anyone.

Appendix
Mountain Meadows Massacre

Avenging the Blood of the Prophets
by Will Bagley

The evidence about who ordered the destruction of the Fancher Party and the brutal murder of 120 men, women and children at Mountain Meadows in 1857 has traditionally supported two interpretations: The orders either came from Salt Lake or from local leaders in southern Utah, who then hid the truth from Mormonism's prophet.

Sixty-three years ago in her classic study, *The Mountain Meadows Massacre*, Juanita Brooks concluded one unfortunate circumstance after another led to the crime. "While Brigham Young and George A. Smith, the church authorities chiefly responsible," she wrote "did not specially order the massacre, they did preach sermons and set up social conditions which made it possible." This indicates that even with the limited information she had, this courageous historian assigned moral responsibility for the crime to Mormonism's highest leaders. Brooks also established "from the most impeccable Mormon sources" that Brigham Young obstructed federal investigations and attempts to prosecute the crime for 18 years. Legally, he was guilty of felony murder, even if he didn't order the crime in the first place.

The simplest explanation of Mountain Meadows is that Brigham Young ordered the massacre for both political and religious reasons. Politically, Young needed "Indian" violence to demonstrate his power to cut communications between the Atlantic and Pacific. If the U.S. sent an army to Utah, he blustered, "travel must stop; your trains must not cross this continent." Young boasted only his influence had restrained Indian attacks on overland emigration, and if war came,

"I will say no more to the Indians let them alone, but do as you please. And what is that? It is to use them up; and they will do it." At Mountain Meadows, Mormons dressed as Indians "used up" an entire wagon train.

Religiously, the massacre fulfilled a temple vow, in which "each and all agree to avenge the blood of the prophets, Joseph and Hyrum, who have sealed their testimony with their blood, this you will teach to your children and your children's children to the third and fourth generations. This you do in the presence of God and ministering angels." This "oath of vengeance" also covered the recent blood of another Mormon prophet, Apostle Parley. P. Pratt, who was murdered in Arkansas, shortly after the Fancher Party left their homes in the northwest corner of the state.

I long ago realized trying to "prove" anything about this appalling crime would only prove I was an idiot. The evidence has been so thoroughly corrupted—suppressed, destroyed, and fabricated—it's hard to determine the date the murders took place, let alone trace all the ins-and-outs of the conspiracy behind the crime. But as any attorney knows, the problem with a guilty client is he acts guilty; after the massacre Brigham Young never behaved like an innocent man. Young's fiery discourses calling for blood and vengeance, his encouragement of Indian attacks on wagon trains, and the countless lies he told to cover-up the crime—all show he was intimately involved in fomenting a vicious act of violence.

Shortly after the outbreak of the Civil War, Brigham Young and his entourage visited Mountain Meadows for the first time since 1857. He stopped at the cairn the First Dragoons had raised in 1859 over the grave of the emigrants whose scattered bones they had collected and buried. Young read the Bible verse the soldiers had inscribed on a cedar cross atop the monument: "Vengeance is mine, saith the Lord."

"It should read," he said, "'Vengeance is mine, and I have taken a little.'" Young did not say, "The Lord has taken a little"; he said, I have taken a little.'" Without a word, Young directed the desecration of the grave. "He just lifted his right arm to the square," recalled massacre participant Dudley Leavitt, "and in five minutes not one stone stood upon another." (Raising your right arm to the square is part of the Mormon temple endowment.) A few days later, Young told John D. Lee "the company that was used up at the Mountain Meadowes" included the fathers, mothers, brothers, sisters "& connections" of the men who murdered the Prophets, and "they Merited their fate." The only thing that ever troubled Young "was the lives of the Women & children, but that under the circumstances [it] could not be avoided."

"But," Mormon historians object, "this is purely circumstantial evidence." Could be, but it's no more circumstantial than the evidence O. J. Simpson murdered his wife.

Why didn't Brigham Young use his powers as territorial governor to hunt down and hang the men who committed this despicable crime? Why did he do *nothing* to return the stolen property of the 17 surviving orphans? Why did he bully and threaten the lives of honest men who called for justice in the matter? Why did he shield the murderers right up to the execution of John D. Lee? Why did he allow the church's newspaper to blame to crime on the Indians for a dozen years after Jacob Hamblin told him Mormons did it? And why do these lies about Mountain Meadows continue to this very day? One last question: why has so much evidence been destroyed or purged from Mormon archives, and why was so much evidence hidden in the church's archives for so long? "The suppressing of evidence," Andrew Hamilton said in 1735, "ought always be taken for the best evidence."

The best evidence shows Brigham Young issued the orders that led to the treacherous murder of some 120 men, women, and children at Mountain Meadows on September 11, 1857.

Will Bagley is an independent historian. Along with historian David L. Bigler, his work on Mountain Meadows has won two John Whitmer Historical Association prizes for Best Book in Latter Day Saint History; two Western Writers of America Spur Awards; the Utah State Historical Society's Amy Allen Price Military History Award; the Denver Public Library's Caroline Bancroft History Prize; Westerners International's Best Book Award; and the Western History Association's Caughey Book Prize for the Most Distinguished Book on the History of the American West.

Further Reading

Will Bagley. *Blood of the Prophets: Brigham Young and the Massacre at Mountain Meadows*. Norman: University of Oklahoma Press, 2002.

David L. Bigler and Will Bagley, eds. *Innocent Blood: Essential Narratives of the Mountain Meadows Massacre.* Norman, Oklahoma: The Arthur H. Clark Company, 2008.

David L. Bigler and Will Bagley. *The Mormon Rebellion: America's First Civil War, 1857–1858.* Norman: The University of Oklahoma Press, 2011.

Evangelicals and the LDS

Relations between evangelical Christians and the LDS have improved somewhat in the last several decades. Prior to that, it would be fair to say that there was coolness or even contempt, owing to the heat of polemics and the proselytizing from both sides. Latter-day Saints claimed to be "the one true Church," and evangelicals accused Mormons of being in a cult. Tensions between evangelicals and Christians reached a peak in 1982 with the release of *Godmakers* (Jeremiah Films), an expose on the LDS from longtime critics Ed Decker and Dick Baer.

The Godmaker Controversy

The *Godmakers* video is probably the most powerful and controversial critique of Mormonism ever produced. It was condemned by Mormons at its release and some liberal Christian groups attacked the video as bigoted and unfair. While the video contains some careless arguments, and the cartoon presentation of Mormon beliefs lacks subtlety, the presentation of what the LDS Church teaches is often quite accurate, though sensationalized. Obviously, many LDS members found the form of the attack unbearable.

The *Godmakers II* video, issued in 1992, contains some major faults that damaged its credibility. The depiction of the Mormon Temple Ceremony is outdated as it does not reflect the major changes made in the temple rituals in April 1990. The video also implies that Lillian Chynoweth, a former member of a split-off fundamentalist Mormon group, was a victim of murder by the Mormon Church. In fact, the evidence suggests that Chynoweth committed suicide.

Godmakers II also errs in a major way in suggesting a link between satanic rituals and Mormonism. This is grossly unfair to Mormons. The testimony of William Schnoebelen in the video should be treated with deep suspicion, given his careless regard for facts in his accounts as ex-Catholic, ex-Satanist, ex-Mormon. Jerald and Sandra Tanner subjected the video to lengthy analysis in their work *Problems in The Godmakers II.*

Evangelical attempts to minister to the LDS Church began in the 1800s. The American Baptist Home Mission Society heard a strong appeal on "The Gospel for Utah" at its May 1884 annual meeting. John D. Nutting founded the Utah Gospel Mission in 1900. Mormonism was also targeted in book form throughout the twentieth century. Among the more significant authors are J.K. Van Balaam (*The Chaos of Cults* 1938), Walter Martin (*Mormonism,* 1957, *Kingdom of the Cults,* 1965, and *The Maze of* Mormonism, 1978), and Anthony Hoekema (*The Four Major Cults,* 1963). Jerald and Sandra Tanner and their Utah Lighthouse Ministry have published many works including *Mormonism: Shadow or Reality* (1963, rev. 2008) and *The Changing World of Mormonism* (1980).

While evangelical churches, mission organizations, and authors continue in witness to the LDS world, there has been a general softening in rhetoric and some indications of strategic changes. On this, the exchange between Craig Blomberg and Stephen Robinson in *How Wide the Divide?* is significant.[1] Most important, the mood has been brought about in part by extensive dialogue between evangelical and LDS leaders and scholars. The evangelical side has been led by Richard Mouw (Fuller Seminary) and David Neff (Christianity Today). John Morehead, a former RLDS member turned evangelical, has also championed a dialogue approach towards Mormons. Greg Johnson of Standing Together (founded 2001) has shaped modern evangelical response to Mormonism through his dialogues with Robert Millet, a BYU professor who is the major Mormon leader relating to evangelicals. Gerald McDeremott has had significant interactions with Millet and other Mormons. As well, Bridget "Jack" Jeffries, a female graduate student, is a significant evangelical voice. She is married to a Mormon and is a graduate of Brigham Young University.[2]

One signal of a new dynamic in evangelical relations with LDS involved Ravi Zacharias, the prominent evangelical apologist, preaching at the Mormon Tabernacle on November 14, 2004. Thousands of

Mormons and evangelicals packed the immense edifice in Temple Square to hear him preach on "Defending Jesus Christ as the Way, the Truth, and the Life." Zacharias argued that Jesus understood the depths of human depravity, that his atonement provides full redemption through grace, and that his resurrection is mankind's only hope. While Zacharias affirmed the doctrine of the Trinity, he did not attack Mormonism.

Before Zacharias spoke, Richard Mouw told the Tabernacle audience that evangelicals have sinned against Mormons by misrepresenting them, adding that he hoped evangelicals would "take part" in the 2005 events marking the 200th anniversary of Joseph Smith's birth. Mouw received intense criticism from various evangelicals, including Sandra Tanner, and he later apologized for causing distress in the evangelical community. Mouw outlines his approach to LDS in his recent book *Talking with Mormons* (Eerdmans, 2012) where he argues that evangelicals should not consider the LDS Church a cult, in spite of serious disagreements in theology. Many evangelical LDS watchers, like Bill McKeever and Tanner, remain much more critical of the LDS Church than Mouw even while accepting his call for honest and loving witness.

Modern Mormon Polygamy

As LDS members know, the 1890 Manifesto did not stop all Mormons from defending and practicing polygamy.[1] Polygamist Mormon groups formed in the 1920s in Utah and Arizona, tracing their ideology back to Joseph Smith, Brigham Young, and to an alleged 1886 revelation by Joseph and Jesus Christ to LDS President John Taylor. The largest contemporary polygamous group is the Fundamentalist Church of Jesus Christ of Latter Day Saints. Warren Jeffs became the leader of the group after the death of his father Rulon T. Jeffs in 2002. Jeffs was convicted in 2011 of child sexual assault and is serving a life sentence. Jeff continues to lead the group, originally based in the twin cities of Colorado City, Arizona and Hildale, Utah, an area once known as Short Creek.[2]

The group also has followers in Bountiful, British Columbia, Canada, led by Bishop James Oler. Former leader Winston Blackmore was ousted by Warren Jeffs and this has produced enormous friction among polygamous Mormons in Bountiful.[3] The FLDS also operates the YFZ (Yearning for Zion) Ranch in Eldorado, Texas where a Temple has been built. The site was raided in April 2008 and 439 children were removed from the FLDS compound. However, a Texas Appeals Court ruled that keeping the children away from their homes was unlawful. Search warrants executed during the raid were declared legal and several convictions have resulted.

The second largest polygamist group is the Apostolic United Brethren, now under the leadership of J. LaMoine Jenson. The group was founded by Rulon Allred (b. 1906) who was murdered in 1977 by two female followers of Ervil LeBaron, another polygamist leader. Ervil was originally linked to the Church of the Firstborn of the Fulness of Times, started by his brother Joel in 1955. Joel excommunicated Ervil in 1971. Ervil then started his own group The Church of the Lamb of God and had his brother killed on August 20, 1972. Ervil died in prison in 1981.The whole tragic saga is covered in Jon Krakauer's famous book *Under the Banner of Heaven*.[4] After Rulon Allred's murder his brother Owen led the Apostolic United Brethren until his death on February 14, 2005.

Other polygamous groups include the True and Living Church of Jesus Christ of Saints of the Last Days, based in Manti, Utah (led by James D. Harmston) and the Latter Day Church of Christ, popularly known as the Kingston Clan. The current leader of the group is Paul Elden Kingston. There are also a large number of Independent Fundamentalists who belong to no one group. Altogether it is estimated that there are about 40,000 Mormon polygamists in the United States.[5]

The Church of Jesus Christ of Latter-day Saints no longer allows polygamy. In light of this, it is easy to forget how strongly polygamy was advanced prior to the 1890 ban. Orson Pratt, a Mormon apostle, had this to say in an 1874 sermon at the semi-annual general conference:

I want to say a few words in regard to the revelation on polygamy. God has told us Latter-day Saints that we shall be condemned if we do not enter into that principle; and yet I have heard now and then (I am very glad to say that only a low such instances have come under my notice,) a brother or a sister say, 'I am a Latter-day Saint, but I do not believe in polygamy.' Oh, what an absurd expression! what an absurd idea! A person might as well say, 'I am a follower of the Lord Jesus Christ, but I do not believe in him.' One is just as consistent as the other. Or a person might as well say, 'I believe in Mormonism, and in the revelations given through Joseph Smith, but I am not a polygamist, and do not believe in polygamy,' What an absurdity! If one portion of the doctrines of the Church is true, the whole of them are true. If the doctrine of polygamy, as revealed to the Latter-day Saints, is not true, I would not give a fig for all your other revelations that came through Joseph Smith the Prophet; I would renounce the whole of them, because it is utterly impossible, according to the revelations that are contained in these books, to believe a part of them to be divine—from God—and part of them to be from the devil; that is foolishness in the extreme; it is an absurdity that exists because of the ignorance of some people. I have been astonished at it. I did hope there was more intelligence among the Latter-day Saints, and a greater understanding of principle than to suppose that any one can be a member of this Church in good standing, and yet reject polygamy. The Lord has said, that those who reject this principle reject their salvation, they shall be damned, saith the Lord; those to whom I reveal this law and they do not receive it, shall be damned."[6]

Timeline of Mormonism

1805 Birth of Joseph Smith on December 23 in Sharon, Vermont

1812 Solomon Spalding writes manuscript about discovery of record of earlier civilization in a hill

1816 Smith family moves to Palmyra, New York

1820 Smith family engaged in "money-digging"—use of magic objects to find buried treasure

1820 Smith receives First Vision from God the Father and Jesus

1822 Smith family moves to Manchester, New York

1823 Ethan Smith publishes *Views of the Hebrews* in New York (second edition in 1825)

1823 Angel Moroni tells Smith of gold plates (Sept. 21) and he goes to the Hill Cumorah the next day and sees plates but is not allowed to take them

1823 Alvin Smith, Joseph's brother, dies

1824 Major revival in Palmyra

1826 Smith arrested for "glass-looking" on March 20

1827 Smith marries Emma Hale (age 22) on January 27

1827 Smith gets gold plates from Angel Moroni at Hill Cumorah (September 22)

1828 Martin Harris takes copy of characters from gold plates to Prof. Charles Anthon at Columbia University in February

1828 Harris loses 116 pages of transcripts of gold plates in June

1829 Oliver Cowdery becomes scribe for Joseph

1829 Translation of *The Book of Mormon* completed

1830 *The Book of Mormon* printed on March 26

1830 The church organized on April 6

1831 Smith and wife move to Kirtland, Ohio, in January-February

1831 Some Mormons move to Independence, Missouri

1831 Smith receives revelation on July 20 that Zion site is to be in Independence, Missouri

1832 Brigham Young joins church on April 9

1832 Smith arrives in Missouri on April 24

1833 Smith completes translation of New Testament on February 2

1833 Word of Wisdom revelation given to Smith on February 27

1833 Mormons subject to mob attacks in Jackson County, Missouri

1833 *Book of Commandments* written, containing revelations to Smith

1834 Eber D. Howe's *Mormonism Unvailed* published

1835 *Doctrine and Covenants* accepted as scripture

1835 Smith acquires Egyptian texts and begins translation

1836 Jesus appears to Smith and Cowdery in Kirtland Temple, along with Moses, Elias, and Elijah (April 3—*D&C*, 110)

1836 Smith reportedly has affair with Fanny Alger

1837 Smith and Sidney Rigdon start Kirtland Safety Society Anti-Banking Company and later are fined for unauthorized banking

1838 Smith starts writing *History of the Church*

1838 Military group known as Danites formed in June to protect Mormons

1838 Sidney Rigdon preaches inflammatory "Salt Sermon" (June 17)

1838 Mormons attacked by mobs in Missouri

1838 Smith arrested and then escapes and flees to Illinois (1839)

1839 Smith and other Mormon leaders travel to Washington, DC

1839 Smith starts teaching on plurality of gods

1840 Smith publically announces baptism for the dead

1841 Smith marries Louisa Beaman, aged 26

1842 Smith joins Masonic Lodge and in May introduces temple ceremonies similar to Masonic ones

1843 Smith starts to translate Kinderhook plates

1843 Smith dictates revelation on plural marriage on July 12

1844 Smith announces candidacy for US president

1844 *Nauvoo Expositor* charges Smith with polygamy

1844 Smith killed on June 27 in gun battle while prisoner in Carthage

1844 Sidney Rigdon excommunicated on September 8

1846 On February 4 Mormons begin trek to Utah

1847 Brigham Young and first group of pioneers enter Salt Lake Valley

1848 Reports of crops saved by flock of seagulls eating crickets

1850 *Deseret News* begins publication in Salt Lake City

1852 First public announcement of doctrine of polygamy

1856 Brigham Young gives Blood Atonement speech

1857 Utah War (ends a year later)

1857 Mountain Meadows Massacre on September 11 (120 Arkansas travelers killed in Utah)

1877 John D. Lee executed for leadership in massacre

1880 John Taylor becomes president of church on October 10

1880 *The Pearl of Great Price* accepted as scripture

1889 Wilford Woodruff becomes LDS president

1890 Manifesto about suspension of polygamy

1893 Salt Lake City Temple dedicated

1896 Utah becomes 45th State

1898 Lorenzo Snow becomes LDS president

1901 Joseph F. Smith becomes LDS president

1904 Reed Smoot hearings in Washington

1918 President Smith receives vision of redemption of the dead (*D&C*, 138)

1918 Heber J. Grant becomes LDS president

1925 Training for Missionaries becomes formalized

1936 Church welfare program is organized

1945 George Albert Smith becomes LDS president

1951 David O. McKay becomes LDS president

1953 Police raid on polygamist community in Short Creek Arizona (July 26)

1958 Bruce McConkie *Mormon Doctrine* published

1964 Jerald and Sandra Tanner publish *Mormonism: Shadow and Reality*

1966 McConkie revises *Mormon Doctrine*

1967 Metropolitan Museum in New York presents LDS church with fragments of papyri once owned by Joseph Smith

1970 Joseph Fielding Smith becomes LDS president

1971 Wesley Walters discovers court documents about Joseph Smith

1972 Harold B. Lee becomes LDS president

1973 Spencer W. Kimball becomes LDS president on December 30

1976 Two revelations added to Mormon canon (become *D&C*, 137–138 in 1981) relating to visions

1978 Revelation lifts ban against blacks holding priesthood

1981 New editions of Mormon scriptures published in September

1985 Ezra Taft Benson becomes LDS president on November 10

1986 Mark Hofmann arrested for forgery and murder related to Mormon documents

1990 Major changes in Temple rituals

1993 Six dissidents excommunicated (September) for skepticism and feminist agendas

1994 Howard Hunter becomes LDS president on June 5

1995 Gordon B. Hinckley becomes LDS president on March 12

1995 "The Family: A Proclamation to the World" published on September 23

1997 Membership reaches 10 million in November

2000 LDS Apostles release their testimonies on "The Living Christ"

2002 Winter Olympics in Salt Lake City

2002 Elizabeth Smart (age 14) kidnapped by Brian David Mitchell on June 5

2003 Smart rescued on March 12

2004 DNA evidence contradicts Mormon claim of link between Natives and Jews

2004 Ravi Zacharias preaches in Mormon Tabernacle

2004 Grant Palmer, author of *An Insider's View of Mormon Origins*, disfellowshipped

2005 LDS Church celebrates bicentennial of birth of Joseph Smith

2008 Thomas Monson becomes LDS president

2008 Texas authorities raid FLDS commune in Eldorado

2011 LDS worldwide membership reaches over 14 million

2011 FLDS leader Warren Jeffs sentenced to life in prison for child sex assault

2012 Randy Bott, BYU prof, makes controversial racial remarks in *Washington Post* (Feb. 28)

2012 Dan Peterson dismissed from Maxwell Institute

2012 Mitt Romney loses campaign for US presidency

Resources for Further Study

Pro-LDS Sites

www.lds.org

www.ldsblogs.org

www.timesandseasons.org

www.fairlds.org

www.bycommonconsent.com

Critic Sites

Utah Lighthouse Ministry: www.utlm.org

Mormonism Research Ministry (Bill McKeever): www.mrm.org

Mormon Central (Michael Marquardt): www.xmission.com/~research/central

Recovery from Mormonism: www.exmormon.org

Watchman Fellowship: www.watchman.org

Institute for Religious Research: www.irr.org

Richard Packham: http://packham.n4m.org/tract.htm

Heart of the Matter (Shawn McCraney): www.hotm.tv and www.bornagainmormon.com

Latayne C. Scott: www.latayne.com

Mormon Infographics: www.mormoninfographics.com

Recommended Reading:
Critical Works on Mormonism

The word critical implies both the sense of negative and important. This first section comprises books in both categories. These works are important and to varying degrees offer a negative assessment of Mormonism or some aspect of its history. The endnotes give extensive reference to works by leading Mormon writers.

Richard Abanes, *One Nation Under Gods* (New York: Four Walls Eight Windows, 2002)

Will Bagley, *Blood of the Prophets: Brigham Young and the Massacre at Mountain Meadows* (University of Oklahoma Press, 2002)

S. I. Banister, *For Any Latter-day Saint* (Star Bible Publications, Fort Worth, Texas 76118)

Francis J. Beckwith, Carl Mosser, and Paul Owen, eds. *The New Mormon Challenge* (Grand Rapids: Zondervan, 2002)

Fawn M. Brodie, *No Man Knows My History* (New York: Alfred A. Knopf, 1977, rev. ed.)

Todd Compton, *In Sacred Loneliness* (Salt Lake: Signature, 1997)

Michael Marquardt, *The Rise of Mormonism: 1816–1844* (Longwood: Xulon, 2005)

Michael Marquardt and Wesley Walters, *Inventing Mormonism* (Salt Lake: Signature, 1994)

Bill McKeever and Eric Johnson, *Mormonism 101* (Grand Rapids: Baker, 2000)

Richard and Joan Ostling, *Mormon America* (San Francisco: HarperSanFrancisco, 1999)

Grant Palmer, *An Insider's View of Mormon Origins* (Salt Lake: Signature, 2002)

David Persuitte, *Joseph Smith and the Origins of The Book of Mormon* (Jefferson: McFarland & Company, 2000)

Simon Southerton, *Losing a Lost Tribe* (Salt Lake: Signature, 2004)

Jerald and Sandra Tanner, *The Changing World of Mormonism* (Chicago: Moody Press, 1980)

Richard Van Wagoner, *Mormon Polygamy: A History* (Salt Lake City, UT: Signature Books, 1986)

Dan Vogel, *Joseph Smith: The Making of a Prophet* (Salt Lake: Signature, 2004)

Endnotes

Foreword

[1] *Teachings of Presidents of the Church: Lorenzo Snow*, LDS Church, 2012, p. 83

[2] See *Changing World of Mormonism*, by Jerald and Sandra Tanner, Moody Press, and *Mormonism-Shadow or Reality?*, Utah Lighthouse Ministry. www.utlm.org

[3] "The King Follett Sermon," *Ensign*, LDS Church, April & May issues 1971

The Mormon Story

[1] For basic data see www.mormonnewsroom.org/facts-and-statistics/

[2] The usual place suggested for the first meeting was a home in Fayette, New York. However, Michael Marquardt argues that Manchester, New York is a better alternative. See *The Rise of Mormonism* (Longwood: Xulon, 2005), pp. 212-252.

[3] For a LDS account of Joseph Smith and Mormon history, see Leonard Arrington and David Bitton, *The Mormon Experience* (Bloomington: University of Illinois Press, 2nd ed. 1992).

[4] For two major biographies of the Mormon prophet, see Richard Bushman, *Joseph Smith: Rough Stone Rolling* (New York: Knopf, 2005) and Fawn Brodie, *No Man Knows My History* (New York: Knopf, rev. ed. 1971).

5 For discussion of the succession crisis in 1844, note Michael Quinn, *The Mormon Hierarchy: Origins of Power* (Salt Lake City: Signature Books, 1994).

6 Young, quoted in Arrington and Bitton, p. 101.

7 John G. Turner's recent biography of Young is a major addition to scholarship. See *Pioneer Prophet* (Cambridge: Harvard University Press, 2012).

8 Will Bagley argues that the blame for Mountain Meadows rests at least indirectly with Brigham Young. See his *Blood of the Prophets* (Norman: University of Oklahoma Press, 2002). Ronald W. Walker, Richard E. Turley Jr., and Glen M. Leonard cover the tragedy in *Massacre at Mountain Meadows: An American Tragedy.* New York: Oxford University Press, 2008. This latter work is very important since it is the work of professing Mormons. Bagley accuses them of minimizing Mormon involvement in the murders. See his review in *Pacific Historical Review* (February 2010), pp. 125-126.

9 The Manifesto is included in Doctrine and Covenants as Official Declaration 1.

10 For the full proclamation go to http://www.lds.org/topics/family-proclamation

11 For various responses to the Romney speech, go to http://www.pbs.org/wnet/religionandethics/episodes/by-topic/mitt-romney-mormonism-and-the-presidency/9800/

12 For an affirmation of LDS exclusivism see Apostle Boyd Packer, "The Only True Church" (October 1985), online at lds.org. Robert Millet gives a nuanced interpretation in his edited volume *No Weapon Shall Prosper* (Salt Lake City: Deseret Books, 2011).

13 Matthew Bowman has helpful discussion on charismatic issues in relation to prophetic authority in *The Mormon People* (New York: Random House, 2012).

14 Bowman ends his book with some illuminating comments about The Book of Mormon musical.

He notes that "the musical's Mormons are genuine, entirely without guile, thoroughly and unbelievably committed to the preposterous notion that their bizarre faith can make people's lives better." (p. 250)

The Mormons of the musical are "a national entertainment, and amusing foil to a satisfied modern and secular society...." (p, 251) James Fenton offers important analysis of the musical in *The New York Review of Books* (July 14, 2011).

[15] For the whole story, consult Steven Naifeh and Gregory White Smith, *The Mormon Murders* (New York: Weidenfeld & Nicolson, 1988) and Linda Sillitoe and Allen Roberts, *Salamander: The Story of the Mormon Forgery Murders* (Salt Lake: Signature, 1989). There is also Robert Lindsey, *A Gathering of Saints* (New York: Simon & Schuster, 1988) and Richard E. Turley, *Victims* (Urbana: University of Illinois Press, 1992).

[16] On the ERA and Sonia Johnson, see Mary Bradford, "All on Fire: An Interview with Sonia Johnson," *Dialogue* (Summer 1981), 27-47 and Martha Sonntag Bradley, *Pedestals and Podiums* (Salt Lake City: Signature Books, 2005).

[17] See Lavina Fielding Anderson, "Freedom of Conscience" in *Dialogue* (Winter 1993), 196-202.

[18] See www.feministmormonhousewives.org

[19] For an overview on LDS and homosexuality, see Ron Schow, Wayne Schow, and Marybeth Raynes, eds. *Peculiar People: Mormons and Same-Sex Orientation* (Salt Lake City: Signature Books, 1991).

[20] See Peggy Fletcher Stack, "Gay Mormon named to key local LDS leadership post in San Francisco," *The Salt Lake Tribune* (September 7, 2011). Online at http://www.sltrib.com/sltrib/news/52486958-78/mayne-gay-lds-ward.html.csp#disqus_thread

[21] See www.affirmation.org

[22] For data on the Swedish Rescue, see http://www.mormonthink.com/swedish-rescue.htm

[23] For a conservative attack on Dehlin see Gregory L. Smith's long essay at www.mormoninterpreter.com and his further essay offering explanation of the controversy surrounding his essay. For typical critique of Smith, see the various posts at www.mormoncurtain.com and www.mormondiscussions.com.

[24] Dehlin gave a lecture at the 2012 Sunstone conference where he expressed his doubts about Book of Mormon historicity and the LDS

Church being the "one true Church." He also stated his hope that "Mormonism is somehow big enough and strong enough to withstand, welcome, and even embrace doubters, strugglers, and heretics like us—flaws and all." Online at http://mormonstories.org/wp-content/uploads/2012/07/Dehlin-WhyIStay-Suntone-2012.pdf On Brooks, see *The Book of Mormon Girl* (New York: Simon & Schuster, 2012).

[25] For information on the project and survey, see http://www.whymormonsquestion.org/

[26] Michael Otterson heads Public Affairs for the LDS Church worldwide. He is an On Faith panelist and blogs at http://newsweek.washingtonpost.com/onfaith/panelists/michael_otterson/ In 2010 the Church hired Jesse Stay as their social media architect.

Joseph Smith and the First Vision

[1] www.josephsmith.net under First Vison tab.

[2] See Joseph Smith, *The Pearl of Great Price*, History, chap. 1.

[3] Gordon B. Hinckley, "What Are People Asking About Us?" *Ensign*, November 1998, 70–71.

[4] Hinckley, interview, *The Mormons*, PBS, April 2007.

[5] Carlos E. Asay, "One Small Step for a Man; One Giant Leap for Mankind," *Ensign*, May 1990, 62.

[6] For the historical data verifying a revival in 1824, not 1820, see H. Michael Marquardt and Wesley P. Walters, *Inventing Mormonism* (Salt Lake: Smith Research Associates, 1994), 15–41.

[7] To read the different accounts given from 1827 onward, see http://mit.irr.org/joseph-smiths-changing-first-vision-accounts.

[8] For a recent defense of the First Vision, see Steven C. Harper, "Suspicion or Trust," in Robert L. Millet, *No Weapon Shall Prosper* (Salt Lake City: Deseret Books, 2011), 63–75). Harper has YouTube videos on the First Vision as well. Richard Bushman tries to bring the various accounts together in *Joseph Smith: Rough Stone Rolling* (New York: Knopf, 2005), 35-41. Bushman is probably the most accomplished historian among LDS members. For a personal memoir about his biography of Smith, see *On the Road with Joseph Smith* (Salt Lake City: Greg Kofford Books, 2007).

9 Oliver Cowdery's history of Mormonism, written with Joseph Smith's help, was published in various issues of the *Messenger and Advocate*, Kirtland, Ohio, December 1834 on. For the quote about the angel see vol. 1, 78–79.

10 See the interview with Martin Harris in *Tiffany's Monthly*, 1859, New York. Available at http://www.irr.org/mit/first-vision/1859-account.html.

11 See report about Harris in John A. Clark, *Gleanings by the Way* (W.J. & J.K. Simon, 1842) at http://mit.irr.org/changing-first-vision-accounts-1827-account-martin-harris-to-rev-john-d-clark

12 Fawn Brodie, *No Man Knows My History*, quoted in Jerald and Sandra Tanner's *The Changing World of Mormonism* (Chicago: Moody, 1997), 149. In a later edition Brodie interacts with newly discovered vision accounts but retains her main argument that the 1820 vision was unknown in the early Mormon world or with critics. See 1977 edition, 408ff. Glass looking/money digging referred to Smith's involvement in the mid-1820s practice of looking for buried treasure through psychic means.

13 His mother noted once: "During our evening conversations Joseph would occasionally give us some of the most amusing recitals that could be imagined. He would describe the ancient inhabitants of this continent, their dress, mode of traveling and the animals upon which they rode; their cities, their buildings, with every particular; their mode of warfare; and also their religious worship. This he would do with as much ease, seemingly, as if he had spent his whole life with them" (Lucy Mack Smith, *Biographical Sketches of Joseph Smith*, first published in 1853, 134).

14 See Wesley Walters, "The Mormon Prophet Attempts to Join the Methodists," at http://utlm.org/onlineresources/josephsmithmethodist.htm. Linda Newell and Valeen Avery discuss the Methodist issue in *Mormon Enigma* (Champaign, IL: University of Illinois Press, 1994), 25. Dan Vogel notes Smith's involvement in Methodism in his *Joseph Smith: the Making of a Prophet* (Salt Lake City: Signature, 2004), 60–63.

15 Oliver Cowdery (with assistance from Joseph Smith Jr) in *Messenger and Advocate*, Kirtland, Ohio, December 1834, 1:3.

[16] The LDS website www.josephsmithpapers.org has the original Doctrine and Covenants text online, and the wording can be verified on page 53.

[17] James B Allen, "The Significance of Joseph Smith's 'First Vision' in Mormon Thought," in Michael Quinn, ed. *The New Mormon History* (Salt Lake City: Signature, 1992), 39. Allen, who is a believing Mormon, goes on to note the large absence of the First Vision among Mormons in the 1830s.

[18] See the concluding essay in Robert L. Millet, *No Weapon Shall Prosper*, 411-19. The subjective element in Mormonism is expressed in Moroni 10:4 in the Book of Mormon: "And when ye shall receive these things, I would exhort you that ye would ask God, the Eternal Father, in the name of Christ, if these things are not true; and if ye shall ask with a sincere heart, with real intent, having faith in Christ, he will manifest the truth of it unto you, by the power of the Holy Ghost." For evangelical Christian analysis see Bill McKeever's comments at http://www.mrm.org/praying-about-bofm.

[19] See the discussion in Jerald and Sandra Tanner, *The Changing World of Mormonism.*

[20] Robert Millet is the leading voice for a softer interpretation of the First Vision as it relates to other churches. See his essay "Reflections on Apostasy and Restoration," in his edited volume *No Weapon Shall Prosper* (Salt Lake City: Deseret Book, 2011).

[21] For documentation on these and other parallel statements, see http://www.mrm.org/we-never-criticize

The Prophet and Buried Treasure

[1] See Jerald and Sandra Tanner's *The Salt Lake City Messenger* (August 1971), p. 2 for an early report on the discovery by Wesley Walters. Also note Marvin S. Hill, " Joseph Smith and the 1826 Trial: New Evidence and New Difficulties," *BYU Studies*, vol 12, winter 1972, p. 223-234.

[2] For an exhaustive analysis of money digging and other magical elements of 19th century America, see D. Michael Quinn, *Early Mormonism and the Magic Worldview* (Salt Lake City: Signature Books,

1998, rev. ed.). William Hamblin has a scathing review of Quinn at FARMS Review (2000), Vol. 12, Issue 2, pp. 225-394.

3 See Wesley Walters, *Joseph Smith's Bainbridge, N.Y. Court Trials* (Salt Lake City: Utah Lighthouse Ministry, 1974, 1977). After Walters and a friend named Fred Poffarl discovered the documents they took them from the courthouse. Mr. Poffarl then transported them to the Yale University Beinecke Rare Book Library. The documents were later returned to the courthouse library. Walters admitted in hindsight that they should have made copies and left the documents behind. (See p. 154). Larry C. Porter makes much of this incident in his "Reinventing Mormonism," *FARMS Review* (1995) Vol. 7, Issue 2.

4 Mormon apologist Jeff Lindsay says as part of his response to the glass looking scandal that "the possibility exists that the documents have been tampered with", Mormon Answers to Common Questions. (See http://www.jefflindsay.com/LDSFAQ/FQ_prophets.shtml#convict)

5 I knew Wes Walters personally and arranged a lecture tour with him in eastern Canada in the early 1980s. He passed away in 1990. He was a person of great integrity and his knowledge of early Mormonism was amazing.

6 Brodie, *No Man Knows My History* (New York: Knopf, 1977), chapter 2 and appendix A.

7 See Kirkham, *A New Witness for Christ in America*, quoted in Jerald and Sandra Tanner, *The Changing World of Mormonism* (Chicago: Moody press, 1980), p. 72. Kirkham devoted 150 pages of his work trying to discredit reports about money digging.

8 Hugh Nibley, *The Myth Makers* (Salt Lake City: Bookcraft, 1961), p. 142.

9 Richard Bushman admits to the money digging in *Joseph Smith: Rough Stone Rolling* (New York: Knopf, 2005), pp. 48-52. For non-LDS analysis, see Michael Marquardt, *The Rise of Mormonism 1816-1844* (Longwood: Xulon, 2005), pp. 53-76 and Richard Abanes, *One Nation under Gods* (New York: Four Walls Eight Windows, 2002),pp. 28-33.

10 This is from the *Evangelical Magazine and Gospel Advocate* (April 9, 1831), p. 120.

[11] Oliver Cowdery to W. W. Phelps, October 1835, "Letter VIII," *Latter Day Saints' Messenger and Advocate* 2 (October 1835): 201.

[12] Dan Vogel, "Rethinking the 1826 Judicial Decision," *Mormon Scripture Studies: An E-Journal of Critical Thought.* Online: mormonscripturestudies.com

[13] John Philip Walker, ed., *Dale Morgan on Early Mormonism: Correspondence and a New History* (Salt Lake City: Signature Books, 1986), 373, n. 44.

[14] Affidavit of Isaac Hale, father-in-law of Joseph Smith, Jr., given at Harmony Township, Susquehanna County, Pennsylvania on 20 March 1834 as printed in "Mormonism," Susquehanna Register, and Northern Pennsylvanian 9 (1 May 1834):1, Montrose, Pennsylvania.

[15] Peter Ingersoll Affidavit, Palmyra, Wayne County. N. Y. Dec 2, 1833. Ingersoll is quoted in Eber D. Howe, *Mormonism Unvailed* (1834), p. 234.

[16] Rev. John A. Clark on the Smith family and money-digging in *Gleanings on the Way* (1842)

[17] Young, *Journal of Discourses* Vol. 19 (June 17, 1877), p. 38.

[18] William Stafford Statement on Joseph Smith Jr. Manchester, Ontario Co. N. Y. (Dec. 8, 1833) in Dan Vogel, ed. *Early Mormon Documents* Vol. 2 (Salt Lake City: Signature Books, 1998),p. 61.

[19] See Bushman, 54. Kerry Muhlestein, like Bushman a brilliant LDS scholar, offers the same lame apologetic about money digging. See his essay in Millet, editor, *No Weapon Shall Prosper, pp. 77-93.*

[20] LDS speakers will mention a seer stone but do not always link it to Smith's money digging. For example, see Russell M. Nelson, "A Treasured Testament," *Ensign,* July 1993, 61. The seer stone used by Smith is in the archives of the LDS Church.

[21] Isaac Hale, New York Baptist Register, June 13, 1834. There are other indications that a magical outlook remained part of Smith's life. For example, in 1974 LDS scholar Reed Durham announced to the Mormon History Association the discovery of a magical object that once belonged to the prophet. "I should like to initiate all of you into what is perhaps the strangest, the most mysterious, occult-like esoteric, and yet Masonically oriented practice ever adopted by Joseph Smith....

All available evidence suggests that Joseph Smith the Prophet possessed a magical Masonic medallion, or talisman, which he worked during his lifetime and which was evidently on his person when he was martyred. His talisman ...can now be identified as a Jupiter talisman." LDS leaders criticized Durham for drawing attention to Smith's occult practice and the scholar issued an apology for possibly hurting the faithful. Durham has since admitted that the evidence linking the talisman to Smith is not as solid as he originally thought. Bushman states that "remnants of the magical culture stayed with him [Smith] to the end." (*Rough Stone Rolling*, p. 51.)

Those Many Wives

[1] Included in the Doctrine and Covenants as Official Declaration 1, originally by LDS President Wilford Woodruff, Salt Lake City, Utah, October 6, 1890. For documents related to polygamy, see B. Carmon Hardy, ed., *Doing the Works of Abraham* (Norman: Arthur H. Clark, 2007). Hardy's *Solemn Covenant* (Urbana: University of Illinois Press, 1991) is also important.

[2] Joseph Smith's polygamy is one of the "sensitive issues" covered in Millet, *No Weapon Shall Prosper*. Richard Bushman provides a very unsatisfying apologetic for Smith's polygamy in his *Joseph Smith: Rough Stone Rolling* (New York: Knopf, 2005).

[3] Brian Hales has completed a three volume study on *Joseph Smith's Polygamy* (Greg Kofford Books). Hales defends the integrity of Smith on polygamy. See his testimony at http://mormonscholarstestify.org/793/brian-c-hales He argues that Smith's marriages to already married women never involved sexual relations but admits that "sexual relations were present in some of the Prophet's plural marriages."

[4] Selected quotations from Brodie, *No Man Knows My History*.

[5] Brian Hales and Don Bradley also view Fanny Alger as a case of plural marriage. See Hales at http://www.josephsmithspolygamy.com/JSWives/FannyAlger.html Bradley's views are in "Mormon Polygamy Before Nauvoo?: The Relationship of Joseph Smith and Fanny Alger," in Newell G. Bringhurst and Craig L. Foster, eds *The Persistence of Polygamy: Joseph Smith and the Origins of Polygamy* (Independence, Missouri: John Whitmer Books, 2010).

[6] Andrew Jenson, "Plural Marriage," *Historical Record* 6. July 1887, 233–34.

[7] Most of Smith's plural marriages began while he was in Nauvoo, Illinois. See George D. Smith, *Nauvoo Polygamy* (Salt Lake City: Signature, 2008).

[8] Compton, *In Sacred Loneliness*, 1.

[9] Smith claimed to have received revelation from God that the Old Testament practice was to be restored. This is shown clearly in the famous revelation on polygamy in Section 132 of Doctrine and Covenants.

[10] Both George D. Smith and Todd Compton give details on how Smith related to each of his plural wives.

[11] Compton, *In Sacred Loneliness*, 80-81.

[12] John C. Bennett, a close confidant of Smith, engaged in "spiritual wifery" in 1842 and Smith had him kicked out of the Mormon Church, tracing polygamy to Bennett and not himself. See Richard Van Wagoner, *Mormon Polygamy* (Salt Lake City: Signature, 1989), 17–40.

[13] Dean C. Jessee, *The Personal Writings of Joseph Smith* (Salt Lake City: Deseret Books, 1984), 539–40.

[14] For text of the vow, see http://wivesofjosephsmith.org/16-SarahAnnWhitney.htm

[15] On the Nancy Rigdon case, see Compton, 239-240.

[16] The blog is Hieing to Kolob. For the posting see http://kolobiv.blogspot.ca/2008/12/why-i-would-totally-have-slept-with.html#more The Mormon blogosphere on Smith's polygamy also contains statements that are quite sexist in nature and demeaning to women. See http://www.ldsfreedomforum.com/viewtopic.php?f=14&p=358102

[17] See Van Wagoner, *Mormon Polygamy*, 19.

[18] William Law claimed that he confronted Smith about a revelation promoting polygamy while there was already a revelation in Mormon scripture against the practice. According to Law, Smith replied: "Oh, that was given when the church was in its infancy, then it was all right to feed the people on milk, but now it is necessary to give

them strong meat." Law said the polygamy issue "gave the finishing touch to my doubts and showed me clearly that he was a rascal." Law, interviewed on March 30, 1887, and reported in *The Daily Tribune*, Salt Lake, July 31, 1887. See Compton, 474-479.

[19] On the story behind the two manifestos, see Van Wagoner, *Mormon Polygamy*, 125–76.

[20] On polygamous Mormonism, see Anne Wilde, "Fundamentalist Mormonism," in Newell Bringhurst and John Hamer, eds., *Scattering of the Saints* (Independence: John Whitmer Books 2007), 258–89 and Brian Hales, *Mormon Polygamy and Modern Fundamentalism* (Salt Lake City: Greg Kofford Books, 2006).

[21] One ex-Mormon wrote about Joseph as sexual predator: "Took me YEARS to finally admit that to myself. It was very difficult, very painful to have to admit; since I had tried to defend the man for dozens of years." See http://mormondiscussions.com/phpBB3/viewtopic.php?f=1&t=10466&start=0&st=0&sk=t&sd=a

The Church and the Prophets

[1] On Joseph's translation, see entry in Robert L. Millet et. al., *LDS Beliefs*, 345–47. Also, note Michael Marquardt, *The Rise of Mormonism 1816–1844* (Longwood: Xulon, 2005), 323–52.

[2] While the fifteen men are each called apostle, prophet, seer, and revelator, Thomas Monson is viewed as "the" prophet in virtue of holding the highest office in the LDS Church. For glowing comments about Monson see www.thomasmonson.com under "Come, Listen to a Prophet's Voice."

[3] For official description of the organization of the LDS Church, see www.lds.org. On the complex history of organizational structure in the early LDS church, see D. Michael Quinn, *The Mormon Hierarchy: Origins of Power* (Salt Lake City: Signature Books, 1994), 1–77.

[4] Spencer E. Kimball, *The Teachings of Spencer W. Kimball*, ed. Edward Kimball (Salt Lake City: Bookcraft, 1995), 494.

[5] This is the only verse in chapter 13. A preface indicates that John the Baptist said he was under the direction of Peter, James and John who would give the Melchizedek priesthood later.

[6] The restoration of this higher priesthood in recorded in chap. 27 of Doctrine and Covenants. Mario S. DePillis notes that claims to be the one true church are usually rooted in apostolic succession, miracles, and/or special revelation. In Smith's case, his authority is rooted in claims to special revelation and apostolic succession under the guise of priesthood authority. See DePillis's essay in *The New Mormon History* (Salt Lake City: Signature Books, 1992), 13–35.

[7] See Quinn, *The Mormon Hierarchy: Origins of Power*, 14–32; Grant Palmer, *An Insider's View of Mormon Origins* (Salt Lake City: Signature Books, 2002), 215–234; and Tanner and Tanner, *The Changing World of Mormonism* , 442–47.

[8] See Marquardt's essay on priesthood restoration at www.xmission.com. Vogel covers the topic in his *Religious Seekers and the Advent of Mormonism* (Salt Lake City: Signature Books, 1988), 97–128.

[9] Whitmer, *An Address to All Believers in Christ*, 64.

[10] Ibid., 49.

[11] LaMar Petersen, *Problems in Mormon Text* (Concord, CA.: Pacific, 1957), 7–8.

[12] Smith, *History of the Church*, 3:297.

[13] Conference report, October 1897, 18–19.

[14] See www.lds.org. Two General Authorities quoted Benson with approval in their talks at the General Conference in 2010.

[15] For primary quotes and analysis of Blood Atonement, see Jerald and Sander Tanner, *The Changing World of Mormonism* (Chicago: Moody Press, 1980), 192-208.

[16] On Adam-God see Tanner and Tanner, 192-208.

[17] Obviously, other churches adopted racist views like the LDS Church. The point is not to argue that Young was unique on his racist views but rather that he led the LDS astray on this matter, as current LDS scholars show. See, for example, Armand Mauss, *All Abraham's Children* (Champaign: University Of Illinois Press, 2003).

Endnotes

The Book of Mormon

[1] "Translated by the Power of God," LDS website: mormon.org/book-of-mormon/

[2] Russell Nelson, "A Testimony of the Book of Mormon," 169th Semiannual General Conference, October 1999.

[3] John W. Welch, "Jesus Christ in the Book of Mormon," *The Encyclopedia of Mormonism* (online at http://eom.byu.edu/ byu.edu).

[4] History of the Church of Jesus Christ of the Latter-day Saints, 4:461

[5] For elaborate defense of The Book of Mormon see the writings of LDS apologists Dan Peterson, John Tvedtnes, William Hamblin, John Welch, Louis Midgley, Stephen Ricks, John Gee, Royal Skousen, John Sorenson, and Hugh Nibley, for example. Their writings can be found at online at fairlds.org, maxwellinstitute.byu.edu, www.shields-research.org and other sites.

[6] On The Book of Mormon's basically orthodox Christian perspective, see Ross Anderson, *Understanding the Book of Mormon* (Grand Rapids: Zondervan, 2009). Anderson, an evangelical pastor in Utah and former LDS, also notes those areas where the Book of Mormon teaching differs from the Bible.

[7] For detail on the estimation of Smith among LDS, see James B. Allen, "Second Only to Christ" (online at http://maxwellinstitute.byu.edu/publications/books/?bookid=47&chapid=262).

[8] The LDS Church numbers fourteen million since 1830.

[9] See Fawn Brodie, *No Man Knows My History*, ch. XIV for details on "Disaster in Kirtland."

[10] On the Kinderhook plates, see the documentation at http://www.mormonthink.com/kinderhookweb.htm

[11] It is puzzling that Robert Millet, himself a great scholar, would argue that Smith's translation is one of "the great evidences" of Smith's divine calling. (See *LDS Beliefs*, p. 347.) For an objective look at Smith's work see the analysis by Michael Marquardt in his *The Rise of Mormonism*, pp. 323-352.

[12] John Kessler is Professor of Old Testament and Hebrew at Tyndale Seminary and his doctorate is from the Sorbonne-Paris IV. I asked him to look at Smith's reading of Genesis 1:1 and evaluate his use of Hebrew. Here is what John wrote me:

> "Smith misreads the Hebrew syntax of Gen 1:1. In his attempt to see this verse as stating that the Chief God called together (or created) the other gods he must:
>
> 1. delete the letter *beth* from the first word, *bereshith* (a deletion for which there is no manuscript support whatsoever)
> 2. read *reshith* as a noun meaning "head"; whereas in reality it means "first point, starting point, beginning, first fruit" (to do this he has to treat the yodh and taw at the end of *bereshith* as some kind of suffix or termination, when in truth they belong to the spelling of the noun).
> 3. read *bara'* as meaning "call together" rather than create (its normal meaning)
> 4. read *'elohim* (God) as the direct object of the verb *'bara'*. This is grammatically impossible since its lacks the particle *'et* which introduces the true direct objects (the heavens and the earth) which immediately follow.
> 5. omit the phrase "the heavens and the earth" in his translation.
>
> Oddly Smith has put plural endings on verbs where the Hebrew is singular, and where he seems to be arguing for a singular subject."

[13] On this episode, see, for example, the interesting essay by Kenneth W. Godfrey, "What is the Significance of Zelph in the Study of Book of Mormon Geography?" Journal of Book of Mormon Studies 8:2 (1999), pp. 70-79, 88.

I realize that various Mormon scholars honestly believe in all such accounts by Smith. I respect their right to do so but believe they have an unwarranted trust in him and the historical accuracy of The Book of Mormon.

[14] For documentation on failed prophecies, see S.I. Banister, *For Any Latter-day Saint* (Fort Worth: Star Bible Publications, 1988), pp. 315-348. Smith's proposed success on predicting the Civil War is a case of overstatement. See the discussion at http://www.mrm.org/civil-war

[15] See *History of the Church*, Vol. 6, p. 408, 409.

[16] For critique of the Witnesses, see the arguments at http://www.irr.org/mit/bom-wit-pt1.html.

[17] Alexander Campbell, *Millennial Harbinger* (February 1831), 93. Available at http://www.truthandgrace.com/1831bomcritique.htm. For detail on anachronisms in the Book of Mormon, see Jerald and Sandra Tanner, *The Changing World of Mormonism* (Chicago: Moody Press, 1979), chap. 5.

[18] Robert Millet, one of the most influential LDS scholars, admits that archaeological support for the Book of Mormon remains something beyond current evidence. See his dialogue with Gregory Johnson in *Bridging the Divide* (Rhinebeck, NY: Monkfish, 2007), 75.

[19] The original 1996 notice which was severely critical of the Mormon scriptures was revised in 1998 to state "The Book of Mormon is a religious document and not a scientific guide, The Smithsonian Institution has never used it in archeological research." Cited in *Journal of Book of Mormon Studies* 7, issue 1 (Provo: Maxwell Institute, 1998): 77.

[20] Letter to the Institute for Religious Research, Grand Rapids, Michigan, August 12, 1998, from the National Geographic Society. Available on the Institute for Religious Research website.

[21] The 1996 notice can be seen at http://www.utlm.org/onlineresources/smithsonianletter.htm.

[22] Simon Southerton, *Losing a Lost Tribe* (Salt Lake City: Signature, 2004). Southerton argues that DNA testing of Native Americans shows Asian ancestry not Middle Eastern. The dominant LDS reply to Southerton rests on the view that the Lamanite and Nephite migration involved only a small group who settled in a limited geographical area of the Americas. See Ugo A. Perego, "The Origin of Native Americans," in Robert L. Millet, ed., *No Weapon Shall Prosper* (Salt Lake City: Deseret Books, 2011), 171–216. Most Mormons through history have believed that the Jewish migrations involved large parts of the Americas, from New York State down into Central America. For a critique of the limited geography perspective see Deanne G. Matheny, in Brent Metcalfe, ed. *New Approaches to the Book of Mormon* (Salt Lake City: Signature Books, 1993), ch. 8.

[23] See a graphical illustration of the change at http://www.mormoninfographics.com/ Also, for a broader analysis of changes see Jerald and Sandra Tanner, *3,913 Changes in the Book of Mormon* (Salt Lake: Utah Lighthouse Ministry, 1996).

[24] Michael Coe, "Mormons and Archaeology: An Outside View," *Dialogue* 8 (Summer 1973): 46.

[25] For detailed evidence, see Stan Larson, "The Historicity of the Matthean Sermon on the Mount in 3 Nephi," in Brent Lee Metcalfe, *New Approaches to the Book of Mormon*, ch. 5.

[26] Grant H. Palmer, *An Insider's View of Mormon Origins* (Salt Lake City: Signature Books, 2002), 82–90.

[27] On the complicated B.H. Roberts case, see the material at http://www.mormonthink.com/josephweb.htm#bh

Doctrine and Covenants

[1] Doctrine and Covenants, Introduction, 6

[2] C. Max Caldwell, "Doctrine and Covenants: Contents" in *The Encyclopedia of Mormonism* (online at http://eom.byu.edu/).

[3] Bill McKeever, *Mormonism 101* (Grand Rapids: Baker, 2000), 124–25.

[4] John A. Widtsoe, *Joseph Smith—Seeker After Truth, Prophet of God*, (Salt Lake City: Deseret News Press, 1952), 119.

[5] *Doctrines of Salvation: Sermons and Writings of Joseph Fielding Smith*, ed. Bruce R. McConkie, vol. 1 (1954), 170

[6] See Richard Van Wagoner, Steven Walkter, and Allen Roberts "The 'Lectures on Faith': A Case Study in Decanonization," *Dialogue* (Fall 1987), 71-77.

[7] Letter written by David Whitmer, published in *The Saints' Herald*, February 5, 1887 (Iowa). A copy of this paper is available online at http://www.sidneyrigdon.com/dbroadhu/IA/sain1887.htm#020587

[8] See Jerald and Sandra Tanner, *The Changing World of Mormonism* (Chicago: Moody Press, 1980), 45.

[9] David Whitmer, *An Address To All Believers in Christ*, Richmond, Missouri, April 1887, 59.

10 Ibid., 61.

11 See for example Jerald and Sandra Tanner's Introduction to 3,913 Changes in the Book of Mormon, Utah Lighthouse Ministry, online: http://www.utlm.org/onlinebooks/3913intro.htm

12 Jerald passed away in 2006. Sandra continues their Utah Lighthouse Ministry. See utlm.org

13 For a brief account of the Tanners' spiritual journey, see *Salt Lake City Messenger* #108 (May 2007) and #109 (October 2007), online at utlm.org.

14 See footnote 11 above.

15 Jerald and Sandra Tanner, *The Changing World of Mormonism*, 43.

16 Michael D. Quinn, "On Being a Mormon Historian (And Its Aftermath)" in George D. Smith, Faithful History: Essays on Writing Mormon History. (Salt Lake City: Signature Books, 1992), 69–111.

17 Ibid., 86. In a postscript to his lecture, Quinn recounts the factors that led to his 1988 resignation from Brigham Young University. Just after his resignation he told a reporter that "BYU is an Auschwitz of the mind." (p. 94)

18 Hugh W. Nibley, *Tinkling Cymbals and Sounding Brass*, vol. 11 in *The Collected Works of Hugh Nibley* (Salt Lake City: Deseret Book and FARMS, 1991), 3–52.

19 McLellin in *The Saints' Herald*, Vol. 17:556- 557, cited in *The Changing World of Mormonism*, 65. For online discussion of McLellin, see Jerald and Sandra Tanner at http://www.utlm.org/online books/changingtherevelations.htm.While Mormon scholars have dealt with the issue of changing revelation, few LDS members would know much about the topic.

The Pearl of Great Price

1 General data on PGP from Kenneth W. Baldridge, "Pearl of Great Price: Contents and Publication," *The Encyclopedia of Mormonism* (http://eom.byu.edu/).

[2] The entire History is available online at http://www.boap.org/ LDS/History/History_of_the_Church/. LDS scholars are preparing a new annotated history.

[3] H. Michael Marquardt, "Joseph Smith's Egyptian Papers: A History," in *The Joseph Smith Egyptian Papyri: A Complete Edition*, ed. Robert K. Ritner (Salt Lake City: Signature Books, 2012). Excerpted online at signaturebooks.com.

[4] For discussion of the Book of Abraham see *History of the Church of Jesus Christ of the Latter-day Saints* 2:235–236; 348–351.

[5] For example, LDS President John Taylor taught in 1881 that "And after the flood we are told that the curse that had been pronounced upon Cain was continued through Ham's wife, as he had married a wife of that seed. And why did it pass through the flood? Because it was necessary that the devil should have a representation upon the earth as well as God." (Journal of Discourses 22:304).

[6] On racism in American Christianity, see Forrest G. Wood, *The Arrogance of Faith* (New York: Knopf, 1990).

[7] "If You Could Hie to Kolob" is hymn no. 84 and was written by William Phelps, an early Mormon leader.

[8] For a signal of the difficulty of interpreting the Book of Abraham, see Daniel Peterson, John Gee, and William Hamblin, "And I Saw the Stars," in Gee and Brian Hauglid, eds. *Astronomy, Papyrus, and Covenants* (Provo: Maxwell Institute, 2006).

[9] For example, Doctrine and Covenants 49:17; Book of Moses 3:5.

[10] Some LDS scholars argue for the continuity of Smith's understanding of God from the Book of Mormon through his translation of the Book of Abraham and to his death. For this perspective see Robert Millet et al., *LDS Beliefs: A Doctrinal Reference* (Salt Lake: Deseret Book, 2011). Other LDS scholars argue that Smith changed his theology. For the latter position, see the influential essay by Thomas Alexander, "The Reconstruction of Mormon Doctrine," *Sunstone* 5:4 (July–August 1980): 24–33.

[11] For a defense of LDS theology as monotheistic, see *LDS Beliefs*, 436-37. The hymn about Kolob noted above has this question in stanza one: "Do you think that you could ever, Through all eternity, Find out the generation, Where Gods began to be?"

The Book of Abraham

1 William W. Phelps, Kirtland, Ohio to Sally Phelps, Liberty, Missouri, 20 July 1835, in *Journal History of the Church*, 20 July 1835. The Phelps letter is quoted widely. See, for example, Michael Marquardt, *The Rise of Mormonism: 1816–1844* (Longwood: Xulon, 2005), 391-92.

2 For images of some of the relevant documents, see http://www.pleaseconvinceme.com/index/Can_We_Trust_the_Book _of_Abraham

3 William S. West, *A Few Interesting Facts Respecting the Rise, Progress and Pretensions of the Mormons* (Warren, Ohio, 1837), 5–6

4 Theodule Deveria, *Memoires et Fragments*, ed. Gaston Maspero, (Ernest Leroux, Paris, France 1896), vi-viii.

5 *Joseph Smith As Translator: An Inquiry Conducted by Rt. Reverend F.S. Spalding, D.D., Bishop of Utah*, (New York: Protestant Episcopal Church, The National Council), 23-24.

6 Ibid, 27.

7 Ibid, 30–31.

8 Ibid, 23.

9 Roberts realized the troubles that would be created if Smith erred on the Book of Abraham. "If Joseph Smith's translation of the Egyptian parchment could be discredited, and proven false, then doubt would be thrown also upon the genuineness of his translation of the Book of Mormon; and thus all his pretensions as a translator would be exposed and come to naught." B.H. Roberts, *A Comprehensive History of the Church* (Salt Lake City: Deseret News Press, 1930), Vol. 2, p. 138.

10 Nancy Ashment, "Why I Am Not a Mormon," interview for Frontline, PBS, April 30, 2007. Online: www.pbs.org http://www.pbs.org/mormons/themes/whyiamnot.html

11 Muhlestein has a defense of the Book of Abraham in Robert L. Millet, ed. *No Weapon Shall Prosper* (Salt Lake City: Deseret Book, 2011).

12 Robert K. Ritner, ed., *The Joseph Smith Egyptian Papyri: A Complete Edition* (Salt Lake City: Signature Books, 2012), 137. In footnote 331 Ritner wrote: "I have no reason to regret my earlier description of his "translations" as "outlandish," "nonsense," "hopeless" and "uninspired fantasies."

[13] Ibid, 143.

[14] See Ritner, *The Joseph Smith Papyri*, 142n358.

[15] Robert K. Ritner, "Scholar Says Mormon Scripture Not an Egyptian Translation," in The *Joseph Smith Egyptian Papyri: A Complete Edition*, (Salt Lake City: Smith-Pettit Foundation of Salt Lake City, 2012). Online: signaturebooks.com.

[16] Palmer, *An Insider's View of Mormon Origins* (Salt Lake City: Signature Books, 2002), 18ff.

[17] For further analysis see Erich Paul, *Science, Religion and Mormon Cosmology* (Bloomington: University of Illinois Press, 1992).

[18] For discussion on changes in editions, see the data at http://www.conchisle.com/pg.htm

[19] See for example Darren Hewer, "Book of Abraham Analysis," on Why Faith? website, 2006. Online: www.whyfaith.com/boa/

[20] Introductory note to the Book of Abraham, on the website of the LDS; classic.scriptures.lds.org/en/pgp/introduction

[21] John Gee, quoted in R. Scott Lloyd, "The Book of Abraham: The Larger Issue," *LDS Church News*, Deseret News Publishing Company, August 11, 2009. Online: ldschurchnews.com

[22] Ibid.

God and Many Gods

[1] The Articles of Faith are now part of the Pearl of Great Price, as noted earlier. The Articles were first written by Joseph Smith in a 1942 letter to a Chicago editor named John Wentworth. See the Mormon newspaper *Times and Seasons* 3:706 (March 1, 1842). The primary issue of the newspaper can be seen at http://www.centerplace.org/history/ts/v3n09.htm

[2] 3 Ne. 13:9, paraphrasing Matt. 6:9.

[3] Jeffrey R. Holland, "The Only True God and Jesus Christ Whom He Hath Sent," October 2007 General Conference. See http://www.lds.org/general-conference/2007/10/the-only-true-god-and-jesus-christ-whom-he-hath-sent?lang=eng.

[4] Ibid.

5 For a defense of classical Christian monotheism see Paul Owen's essay in Francis Beckwith, Carl Mosser and Paul Owen, eds. *The New Mormon Challenge* (Grand Rapids: Zondervan, 2002), 271–314.

6 Abraham 3:15; 4:3, 10, 25; 5:8.

7 "King Follett" sermon, *Journal of Discourses* 6:5.

8 "Sermon in the Grove," preached June 16, 1844. *History of the Church* 6:473–79; *Teachings of the Prophet Joseph Smith*, 369–76. Available from http://emp.byui.edu/jexj/courses/sermon_in_the_grove.htm .

9 Ibid.

10 *Journal of Discourses*, 2:345.

11 *Ibid.*, 7:333.

12 This verse is central in a campaign by Mormonism Research Ministry to highlight the orthodox view of God in the Book of Mormon. See www.weagreewith818.com

13 Thomas Alexander is the most well-known LDS scholar who argues for development in Smith's view. See his comments on his influential 1980 essay making this point in *Sunstone* 112 (December 1999), 24–29.

14 "King Follett Discourse," *Journal of Discourses* 6:3–4, also in *Teachings of the Prophet Joseph Smith*, 342–45. Available from http://emp.byui.edu/jexj/courses/sermon_in_the_grove.htm.

15 For powerful biblical and philosophical critique of the Mormon understanding of creation and God, see Carl Mosser and Paul Owen, eds., *The New Mormon Challenge*, 95–218. Paul Copan and William Lane Craig defend creation ex nihilo. Jim Adams argues that Mormonism is inconsistent with Old Testament teaching. Stephen Parrish and Carl Mosser critique the Mormon view of God. Also, see Francis Beckwith and Stephen Parrish, *The Mormon Concept of God* (Lewiston: Edwin Mellon, 1991).

16 J. P. Moreland defends the traditional Christian view that God is immaterial in Mosser and Owen, *The New Mormon Challenge*, 243–66.

17 In the 1990s Janice Allred and Gail Houston were each disciplined for dealing with the Heavenly Mother concept in ways the LDS Church did not approve. Houston was fired from Brigham Young

University. Allred left the Church and wrote *God the Mother* (Salt Lake City: Signature, 1997).

[18] See David Paulsen and Martin Pulido, "A Mother There," *Brigham Young University Studies* 50, 1 (2011), 70–126. Belief in Heavenly Mother is also affirmed in Millet et al., *LDS Beliefs*, 440–41. Note Linda Wilcox, "The Mormon Concept of a Mother in Heaven," *Sunstone* 112 (December 1999), 78–87. This is a reprint of her 1980 article with added commentary.

[19] The issue is taken up on the website www.godneversinned.com

Jesus, Holy Spirit and Humanity

[1] See the entries on "Atonement, Miracles, and Resurrection" in Miller et al., *LDS Beliefs*.

[2] For the case for a high christology, see Murray Harris, *Jesus as God* (Grand Rapids: Baker, 1998).

[3] Robert R. Millet et al., *Bridging the Divide* (Rhinebeck, NY: Monkfish Book Publishing, 2007), 83.

[4] See "Names of God" in Walter A. Elwell, ed., *Baker's Evangelical Dictionary of Biblical Theology* (Grand Rapids: Baker, 1996).

[5] Lecture 5 deals with the Father, Son, and Spirit. The text states that the Father and Son possess "the same mind" which is "the Holy Spirit." The Lectures were part of the original Doctrine and Covenants published in 1835.

[6] For a viewpoint of the confusing aspects of LDS teaching on the Holy Spirit, see Tanner and Tanner, *The Changing World of Mormonism*, 188–90. Joseph Fielding Smith, the nephew of the founding prophet dismissed the idea that the Holy Spirit might be a woman. See Smith, in *Changing World*, p. 189.

[7] Millet has authored many works including *The Mormon Faith* (Salt Lake City: Shadow Mountain, 1998) and *Grace Works* (Salt Lake City: Deseret Book, 2003).

[8] *Grace Works*, 13.

[9] See the entry on "Gethsemane" in Miller, *LDS Beliefs*, 254–58.

[10] For LDS emphasis on works, see "Grace" in Bill McKeever, *In Their*

Own Words (Draper: Mormonism Research Ministry, 2009). Like Millet, Stephen Robinson, another BYU professor, has emphasized salvation by grace. See his *Believing Christ* (Salt Lake City: Deseret Book, 1992).

[11] See Clyde J. Williams, ed., *The Teachings of Lorenzo Snow* (Salt Lake City: Bookcraft, 1984), 1.

[12] Don Lattin, "Musings of the Main Mormon," *San Francisco Chronicle*, April 13, 1997.

[13] Gordon B. Hinckley, quoted in Richard N. Ostling, "Kingdom Come," in *Time*, August 4, 1997, 56. A LDS spokesperson said that the prophet's words were taken out of context, but the *Time* reporter (Richard Ostling) provided a transcript of the interview and his reporting looks accurate. The Mormon organization FAIR tried to show that Time magazine got it wrong but still acknowledged that the emphasis in LDS teaching is on man's present and not "Heavenly Father's past."

[14] See, for example, Blake T. Ostler, "Re-Visioning the Mormon Concept of Deity," *Element* 1, no. 1, (Spring 2005). Online at www.smpt.org.

[15] Joseph Smith, History of the Church of Jesus Christ of the Latter-day Saints 6:305.

[16] *Gospel Principles* (online at lds.org), see chap. 47: "Exaltation," p. 280 in print version.

[17] Some Mormon thinkers are drawing parallels to the way that the Eastern Orthodox Church speaks of humans becoming divine. See Millet, *Getting at the Truth* (Salt Lake City: Deseret Book, 2004), 112–16 and Stephen Robinson in *How Wide the Divide?* (Downers Grove: InterVarsity, 1997), 80–82.

The Temple and the Secrets

[1] Hugh Nibley, "Meaning and Function of Temples," *The Encyclopedia of Mormonism* (online at http://eom.byu.edu/index.php/Temples) Nibley writes: "Here time and space come together; barriers vanish between this world and the next, between past, present, and future."

[2] The history of the LDS and other Mormon groups in relation to temple sites in Missouri is explored in Craig S. Campbell, *Images of the New Jerusalem* (Knoxville: University of Tennessee Press, 2004).

[3] Richard Packham has written quite extensively about temple ceremonies and changes in wording and practice over the decades. See http://packham.n4m.org/temples.htm In 2012 the entire endowment ceremony was filmed and put on YouTube. Obviously, this created hurt and anger among LDS since they regard the ceremonies as sacred. One clear advantage for LDS in the public record of the ceremony is that there is no worship of Satan/Lucifer, thus refuting some extreme accusations in that regard.

[4] The Word of Wisdom is a revelation received by Joseph Smith on February 27, 1833. It is recorded in Doctrine and Covenants, section 89. See the entry on "Word of Wisdom" in Millet et. al., *LDS Beliefs*.

[5] For practical details on temple administration, see "Mormon Temples: How They Work" at www.bycommonconsent.com. The five-part series is the work of W.V. Smith, a mathematics professor at Brigham Young University.

[6] See Todd Compton, *In Sacred Loneliness* (Salt Lake City: Signature, 1997), 8.

[7] On the Lucinda Harris case, note the discussion of Brian Hales at http://www.josephsmithspolygamy.com/JSPolyandry/MASTERSexual Polyandry.html

[8] For text of the sealing ceremony see http://www.lds endowment.org/sealing.html. The website is the creation of a faithful LDS member who believes that sensitive disclosure of temple ritual is the proper answer to rumor and speculation.

[9] See www.mormonnewsroom.org

[10] Brigham Young, Journal of Discourses 2:315. Sermon on April 6, 1853.

[11] For wording on the temple ceremony, see http://packham.n4m.org/endow90.htm. For a printed version, see Jerald and Sandra Tanner, *Evolution of the Mormon Temple Ceremony 1842–1990* (Salt Lake City: Utah Lighthouse Ministry, 1990).

[12] See *History of the Church* 4:208. The August 2001 LDS *Ensign* magazine quotes Smith: "Ordinances instituted in the heavens before the foundation of the world, in the priesthood, for the salvation of man, are not to be altered or changed." (22) For documents related to the temple, see Devery Scott Anderson, ed., *Development of LDS Temple Worship 1846–2000* (Salt Lake City: Signature, 2011).

[13] This statement is from W. Grant Bangerter, at the time executive director of the Temple Department in Salt Lake City. See *Deseret News*, Church Section, January 16, 1982.

[14] For details see David John Buerger, *The Mysteries of Godliness: A History of Mormon Temple Worship* (San Francisco: Smith Research Associates, 1994). I have also drawn from the timeline and detail at www.ldsendowment.org.

[15] For a color-coded documentation of changes between the 1990 ceremony and its predecessor, go to http://www.i4m.com/think/temples/temple_ceremony.htm.

[16] For the whole dialogue see the relevant section at http://www.ldsendowment.org/1931.html.

[17] See Michael Homer, "Similarity of Priesthood in Masonry," *Dialogue* (Fall 1994) and Buerger, *The Mysteries of Godliness*, 44–58. Homer is working on a definitive study of the relationship of Masonry to Mormonism.

[18] See the comments at http://www.exmormon.org/templex.htm One ex-Mormon states: "where was Jesus? Why wasn't he the star of the show?"

Blacks and the Priesthood

[1] See Official Declaration 2 in Doctrine and Covenants.

[2] For a moving account behind the Declaration, see Edward Kimball, "Spencer W. Kimball and the Revelation on Priesthood," *BYU Studies*, 47, no. 2 (2008), pp. 4-78.

[3] See ldsnewsroom.org for both the general statement and the one on Bott.

[4] See Jason Horowitz, "The Genesis of a church's stand on race," *Washington Post* (February 28, 2012).

[5] Various Mormon blogs noted the irony of Bott being criticized by his own Church for using prior Church explanations for the ban against blacks holding the priesthood. See exmormon.org and bycommonconsent.com for example. One blogger notes: "The Church has denounced racism but not a racially based ban. Even the most recent statement, one of the most forceful, simply says (somewhat disingenuously) that we don't know the reason for the ban. Given that the ban itself has never been denounced that leaves room for members of the Church to continue to try to justify it. Is anyone shocked that Brother Bott did just that? Sadly, for whatever reason and despite urging the Church won't just say, "The ban was wrong." (http://bycommonconsent.com/2012/03/01/bott-ulism-outbreaks-and-protective-correlation/)

[6] The Book of Moses 7:2 states that the seed of Cain is "black." The Book of Moses is part of the LDS scripture Pearl of Great Price.

[7] See the discussion at http://mormonitemusings.com/tag/washington-post/ and http://exmormon.org/d6/drupal/Mormon-Brother-Botts-BYU-Briefing-aBout-Blacks-Brews-Big-Brouhaha

[8] For general treatments of racism, see Forrest G. Wood, *The Arrogance of Faith* (New York: Knopf, 1990), Stephen R. Haynes, *Noah's Curse: The Biblical Justification of American Slavery* (New York: Oxford University Press, 2002); David M. Goldenberg, *The Curse of Ham* (Princeton, N.J.: Princeton University Press, 2003); and Benjamin Braude, *Sex, Slavery, and Racism* (New York: Alfred Knopf, 2005).

[9] For analysis of the LDS history on racism, see Armand Mauss, *All Abraham's Children* (Bloomington: University Of Illinois Press, 2003), Newell Bringhurst and Darron Smith, eds. *Black and Mormon* (Bloomington: University Of Illinois Press, 2006), and Jessie L. Embry, *Black Saints in a White Church* (Salt Lake City: Signature Books 1994)

[10] Some writers use the spelling Able. On his specific case see Newell Bringhurst's essay in *Neither White Nor Black* (Salt Lake City: Signature Books, 1984), online at http://signaturebookslibrary.org/?p=449

Endnotes

Conclusions

[1] While Emma was upset by her husband's breaking of their wedding vows it remains uncertain whether she tried to poison him late in their marriage. See Linda King Newell, "The Emma Smith Lore Reconsidered," in *Dialogue* Vol. 17, no. 3 (1989).

[2] Smith's failures in prophecy as well as those of other Mormon prophets are cause for suspicion of the famed "White Horse" prophecy. See discussion at http://www.mrm.org/white-horse-prophecy

[3] There is little doubt of Smith's influence on the work of the Danites, the Mormon group involved in conflicts in Missouri. On the Danites, note Michael Quinn, *The Mormon Hierarchy* (Salt Lake City: Signature Books, 1994).

[4] See data at http://exmormon.org/d6/drupal/Mormon-Cosmology

[5] The endowment ceremony adopts a rather strange understanding of Elohim, Jehovah and Michael in the narration of Creation and Fall.

[6] The inability of LDS apostles to face issues is shown in the communication between Jeffrey Holland (Quorum of the Twelve Apostles) and Tom Phillips, a former Stake President. The two had been friends. However, Tom's detailed queries about errors were met with evasion by Holland. See http://mormonthink.com/tomphillips.htm for details. Phillips also has a fascinating report at Mormon Think on his Second Anointing.

[7] The LDS Church would be a better movement if the Salt Lake hierarchy listened more closely to those LDS scholars who possess great integrity on historical, moral and theological issues. This applies to the past as well. Armand Mauss was writing with wisdom and courage on racial issues many years ago. He was ahead of the prophets. LDS scholars need to have the courage to speak truth to the Brethren. In this regard, Richard Bushman has a particular responsibility given his enormous learning and status in the world of scholarship. It would also help if Robert Millet would be more precise at places in his explanation of LDS doctrines. For example, in *Modern Mormonism* (Salt Lake: Greg Kofford Books, 2010) he missed the chance to speak definitively against the notion that God the Father is an exalted Man.

Instead, he writes: "what do we know of a time before God was God? Nothing!" It would have been nice to read Millet stating that since God is eternal and is not a man, there was no time before God was God. Millet quotes Hinckley's famous statement on the Lorenzo Snow couplet without acknowledging Hinckley's double-talk on the subject. (p. 4)

[8] See Grant Palmer's helpful comments on how feelings can be misleading in his *An Insider's View of Mormon Origins*, pp. 130-133.

[9] Grant Palmer has been told directly by a member of the First Quorum of the Seventies that unbelief exists at that level of leadership and also even higher in the Salt Lake apostleship.

[10] For an account of a woman who was willing to leave her work at Brigham Young University and Mormon life, see the testimony of Lynn Wilder. See http://www.exmormonscholarstestify.org/lynn-wilder.html

[11] Grant Palmer can be helpful here since he places great stress on Jesus Christ in his developing views since he was forced out of the LDS Church. See his book *The Incomparable Jesus* (Salt Lake: Greg Kofford Books, 2005).

[12] It is curious how LDS leaders have such a harsh view of the failings of other churches but often turn a blind eye about their own tradition. On this double standard, see a similar point made about Jehovah's Witnesses in my book *Crisis of Allegiance* (Burlington: Welch, 1986), p. 94.

[13] On the case for Jesus, see works by Gary Habermas, Alvin Plantinga, William Lane Craig, C.S. Lewis, among others. For a defense of Christian faith in relation to other faiths, consult my *Nelson's Illustrated Guide to Religions* (Nashville: Thomas Nelson, 2009). The case for Jesus does not depend on biblical inerrancy or solving every problem passage in Christian Scripture.

[14] A revised Temple ceremony could place proper emphasis on the Cross rather than Gethsemane as the focal point of redemption.

[15] As another example of the weaknesses of historicity of the Book of Mormon, note the case of Stephen Burnett, an early Mormon. See http://blog.mrm.org/2012/04/mormonism-fell-a-heap-of-ruins/

16 In March 2013 the LDS Church announced a new edition of the English scriptures. The introduction to the Book of Abraham is now said to be "an inspired translation of the writings of Abraham." The addition of the word "inspired" probably indicates awareness that it is not a translation in the regular meaning of the word. Other changes in the 2013 edition involve Doctrine and Covenants. For further detail see http://www.lds.org/bc/content/shared/content/english/pdf/scriptures/approved-adjustments_eng.pdf

17 The idea promoted in LDS literature that Joseph Smith has a role in whether or not anyone gets to the highest heaven is lamentable. Smith's railings against belief in one God near the end of his life are singular proof that he is basically a false teacher. His complaints about the Trinity idea are rather hollow in light of his advocacy of humans as Gods. To get an idea of how much late Mormonism under Smith departed from the early Mormonism under Smith, see Charles Harrell, *This Is My Doctrine* (Salt Lake: Greg Kofford Books, 2011).

18 Given Joseph Smith's immorality and the ways his leadership led to such ruination among his own followers, it is astonishing that he was proclaimed "King on earth" by the Council of Fifty, a secret group that adopted Smith's theocratic outlook. For the sake of honesty and historical transparency, the First Presidency would do well to release all material about the Council in the LDS archives.

19 Johnstun also has uncovered proof of two new wives for Joseph Smith, one of them quite young. Some of his new discoveries will be presented in a forthcoming work on Joseph H. Jackson, onetime Mormon compatriot to Joseph Smith. Johnstun has already published on Smith's tomb. See *Mormon Historical Studies*, 5:2 (Fall 2005), pp. 163-180.

20 Smith's errors and failings are so constant and significant that he cannot be trusted as a source for Christian truth unless those views are backed by the Bible or by reason. This applies to issues like pre-existence, other worlds, Heavenly Mother, exaltation, three heavens, etc.

21 How can evangelical Christians help the Latter-day Saints? The answer is two-fold. First, evangelical witness to Mormons must be self-critical. It is hypocritical to note weaknesses in Mormon life and faith without doing the same for the evangelical tradition. Second, evangelical Christians should repudiate every popular falsehood said about

Mormons. All in all, evangelical Christians have been careful in critique but there is occasional careless thought and meanness. Though rare, evangelical claims that Mormons worship Lucifer in the Temple are false.

The evangelical-Mormon dialogue has been one of the significant new realities in both traditions. In my opinion, continued dialogue will be enhanced in a major way by more clarity from the LDS Church and its top leaders both about the issues raised in this and other critiques and about what the LDS Church truly believes. For example, questions like "is there really only one God?" or "is God really eternal?" have to be asked simply because of contradictory claims in Mormon scripture or by Joseph Smith or by more recent LDS prophets. Dialogue is only enhanced by laying the cards on the table. To that end, I urge evangelical leaders like Richard Mouw to be somewhat tougher on issues. For example, in his January 2013 conversation with Robert Millet at Calvin College Mouw should have pressed the famous LDS scholar on the controversial Lorenzo Snow couplet. As Sandra Tanner notes in the Foreword in this book, the LDS Church cannot seem to really get away from views said to have been abandoned.

Evangelicals and the LDS

[1] The book was published by InterVarsity in 1997. For an important analysis see Bill McKeever and Eric Johnson at www.mrm.org

[2] Ms. Jack blogs at http://www.clobberblog.com/

Modern Mormon Polygamy

[1] For a general survey from Joseph Smith to the present, see Richard Van Wagoner, *Mormon Polygamy* (Salt Lake City: Signature Books, 1989).

[2] For a journalistic account of Warren Jeffs and his group, see Stephen Singular, *When Men Become Gods* (New York: St. Martin's Press, 2008). For ex-FLDS accounts, see Carolyn Jessop, *Escape* (New York: Broadway Books, 2007) and Brian Mackert, *Illegitimate* (Colorado Springs: David C. Cook, 2008).

[3] The Bountiful Mormon community is covered in Daphne Bramham, *The Secret Lives of Saints* (Toronto: Random House, 2008).

4 Jon Krakauer, *Under the Banner of Heaven* (New York: Anchor, 2004).

5 Anne Wilde, a major leader among Independent Fundamentalists, provides an overview of the major polygamous groups in Newell G. Bringhurst and John C. Hamer, eds. *Scattering of the Saints* (Independence: John Whitmer Books, 2007), 258-289. Brian Hales, a LDS member, surveys the various groups in *Modern Polygamy and Mormon Fundamentalism* (Salt Lake City: Greg Kofford Books, 2006).

6 For Pratt's sermon go to http://scriptures.byu.edu/jod/jodhtml. php?vol=17&disc=34

CASTLE QUAY BOOKS

OTHER AWARD WINNING CASTLE QUAY TITLES INCLUDE:

Bent Hope (Tim Huff)

The Beautiful Disappointment (Colin McCartney)

The Cardboard Shack Beneath the Bridge (Tim Huff)

Certainty (Grant Richison) - NEW!

Dancing with Dynamite (Tim Huff) - NEW! 2011 Book of the Year Award!

Deciding to Know God in a Deeper Way (Sam Tita) - NEW!

The Defilers (Deborah Gyapong)

Father to the Fatherless (Paul Boge)

Find a Broken Wall (Brian Stiller) - NEW!

Hope for the Hopeless (Paul Boge) - NEW!

I Sat Where They Sat (Arnold Bowler)

Jesus and Caesar (Brian Stiller)

Keep On Standing (Darlene Polachic)

The Leadership Edge (Elaine Stewart-Rhude)

Leaving a Legacy (David C. Bentall) - NEW!

Making Your Dreams Your Destiny (Judy Rushfeldt)

Mentoring Wisdom (Dr. Carson Pue) - NEW!

Mere Christian (Michael Coren)

One Smooth Stone (Marcia Lee Laycock)

Predators Live Among Us: Protect Your Family from Child Sex Abuse
(Diane Roblin-Lee) - NEW!

Red Letter Revolution (Colin McCartney)

Reflections (Cal Bombay) - NEW!

Seven Angels for Seven Days (Angelina Fast-Vlaar)

Stop Preaching and Start Communicating (Tony Gentilucci) - NEW!

Through Fire & Sea (Marilyn Meyers)

To My Family (Diane Roblin-Lee)

Vision that Works (David Collins)

Walking Towards Hope (Paul Boge)

What Happens When I Die (Brian Stiller) - NEW!

The Way They Should Go (Kirsten Femson)

You Never Know What You Have Till You Give It Away (Brian Stiller)

For a full list of all Castle Quay and BayRidge book titles visit
www.castlequaybooks.com

12/13

CPSIA information can be obtained at www.ICGtesting.com
Printed in the USA
LVOW12s2327011213

363458LV00017B/785/P